One Union

Many Voices

The EU meets the people

Edited by Anders Samuelsen

Published by
Anders Samuelsen
Rue Wiertz 60, ASP 10G 107
B-1047 Brussels
Belgium

For further information regarding any aspect of this publication, please contact: asamuelsen@europarl.eu.int

ISBN 90-81010-31-X

Table of Contents

Table of Contents – cont.

Foreword

My first year in the European Parliament is over. It has been an eventful year, and I have learnt a lot. This book has been part of the learning process. Fifteen competent analysts and writers have enabled me – as well as the reader – to gain a deeper insight into the challenges that are facing Europe and its nation states. Based on these articles, I have written my own version of a possible way forward and so bring closure to my first year as part of the EU system.

The book has not been written without help, suggestions, encouragement and corrective reading and much more from a key group of people. A special thank you to Emil Kongshøj Larsen and Ditte Steen who have been immeasurably helpful during my first year and were a deciding factor in turning the idea of the book into a reality. People such as these are hard to find. Thank you for allowing yourselves to be moved to Brussels. Thank you to Helge Simmelsgaard because you are always there and have been for the last ten years, as tutor and much more.

Also a big thank you to Dorthe Lange who joined us at the office during the last six months. Her combination of vocational aptitude and a great sense of humour has been invaluable.

Outside of the office I should like to say thank you to each author for their well-disposed attitude towards the project, to Gyldendal, to the Social Liberal supporters 'Fremsyn', to Peter Ludlow (EuroComment), to my sister, Mette Bock, for yet again assisting her little brother by word and deed, and to Lykke Friis and Peter Nedergaard.

And last but not least, thank you to my family, Laila, Mikkel and Emil, whose patience I have now abused for another year.

Anders Samuelsen
August 2005

Introduction

Yes, no, maybe - but what was the question?

The idea behind this book came to me shortly after I became a member of the European Parliament. I was struck by the differing approaches to Europe, not just amongst the 'old' members, but also amongst both the 'new' and those waiting at the door. Whilst some countries view enlargement as a means to greater security and wealth, others see it as a threat to their identity and unity. The issue of enlargement is one of many where a particular country's history, national identity, and culture affect its approach to the EU. But we do not fully understand each other's backgrounds, and the debate is characterised by this. However well equipped we are to understand our own national debates on European issues, we really know little about the views of other countries. This book aims to remedy that. The 15 chapters of the book describe the 15 countries' various motives for entering into the collaboration and the level of their interest in being players of the European Union.[1]

The recent debate on the European Constitution has only made the book more relevant. Member States and populations have reacted very differently to the proposed Constitution. In some countries, referendums were held amid fervent discussion, whilst in others the treaty was agreed upon at parliamentary level without further ado. The result of the Spanish vote was an overwhelming 'yes', but in France and the Netherlands, the majority voted against the Constitution. The crisis which followed these two rejections, revealed yet again our lack of understanding of each other's approach to the European project. This makes progress difficult. The arguments that precipitated the 'no' in France would seem to support a 'yes' in the UK, and increasingly the major countries are pulling in opposite directions in order to secure an EU which their populations will accept. What should have been a clearing out of a mess of treaties and decision-making following the admission of ten new countries has brought a hitherto

---

[1] The 15 authors were given the same task at the same time, although their deadlines varied according to their national circumstances. Where there have been referendums, the authors have had the chance to describe the entire process and comment on the result. All the authors were asked to describe the influence of the no-votes in the Netherlands and France on the national debate in their own country. They were also asked, as their main objective, to look back and describe the political situation at home. The French chapter, like my own, also looks ahead to the future and is suggestive as to how we might move on.

unseen crisis upon the Union. The Constitution, which was aimed at ensuring greater openness and democracy in the EU, and was meant to strengthen citizen's rights, has been rejected, and with it, our enthusiasm has vanished.

But why is this? What were the issues and arguments that shaped the debate? Were these the same across all the Member States, or were there marked differences? What part was played by the various peoples' national identities, and what was the role of the countries' domestic policies? Why did only some countries allow their populations to vote, and did those populations know what they were voting for? Are referendums part of the problem? And last but not least, how do we proceed from here?

These are some of the questions that this book seeks to explore – not by giving final and all-encompassing explanations, but by giving the reader an insight into other countries' debates, or lack thereof.

To understand the 15 countries' motives and backgrounds, and to present them briefly, needs some assistance. Fifteen of Europe's most competent analysts were each asked to contribute a chapter. The 15 countries are made up of four of the original founding states (France, Germany, the Netherlands and Italy), seven from those Western European countries which have since acceded (Denmark, the United Kingdom, Ireland, Portugal, Spain, Austria and Sweden) and finally four of the countries which, due to the cold war, could not be admitted until after the fall of the Berlin Wall (Poland, the Czech Republic, Hungary and Finland). Admittedly, it would have been interesting to include the remaining ten countries, and possibly also those who may soon join (Romania, Bulgaria, Croatia, the West Balkans, Turkey and the Ukraine). This may be the subject for another book. For this one I have attempted to deal with a representative selection of countries.

The 15 chapters form the backdrop to my own analysis and conclusions. These are naturally my own opinions and only I can be held responsible or accountable for them. But based on the 15 contributions to this book, I offer my own tentative suggestions as to a possible way forward. But first, I will be looking at why only some countries chose to hold a referendum.

Asking the people

National referendums regarding EU issues are nothing new. But the no-results in France and the Netherlands have marked a hiatus in a decision-making process hitherto unseen by the EU. In the wake of the Rome summit of October 2004, when 25 heads of state signed the draft of the constitutional treaty, it looked as though ten countries would be holding referendums. This included the Netherlands where there has been no referendum for more than 200 years! To talk of a domino effect would be to exaggerate, but it is clear that one head of state's decision to hold a referendum may have put pressure on others.

If all these proposed referendums had taken place, countries with 247 million European citizens would have been given the chance to express their opinion directly, whilst countries with 210 million citizens would not have been asked.[2]

The articles in this book create a varied picture of the reasons why some countries chose to hold referendums, whilst others were content to let their parliaments ratify the constitutional treaty.

For several of the countries, it is clear that their immediate domestic political situations, rather than ideologies and theoretical considerations, were the deciding factors as to whether the decision was put to a popular vote. In the chapter on the United Kingdom, Jonathan Steele pushes this to its logical conclusion: "When governments and opposition parties promise referendums on Europe, they do it as a way of embarrassing their rivals or scoring points for themselves."

France, Sweden and the Czech Republic are among those countries considered in this book, where – like the UK – domestic political considerations were particularly central to the decision as to whether to hold a referendum. The chapters on these countries give the impression that the decision could have been different had the constitutional treaty been completed two years earlier, or indeed later.

In the UK, Tony Blair's promise of a referendum was most untraditional for a self-professed pro-Europe leader known to have his finger on the pulse of the voters. British voters are notoriously sceptical towards further European integration, and convincing them of the blessings of the constitutional treaty never looked like an easy task. During the last 50 years, there has only been one referendum – when the British agreed to stay in the EC a year after their admission. The British voters were not consulted when entering the EC in the first place, nor during the Maastricht and Amsterdam debates. Just as Blair had earlier promised the British public that they could say their piece if Britain was to give up the pound, the promise of a referendum on the constitutional treaty provided him with a way to rob the EU-sceptical Conservatives of a party-political issue, leaving an awkward decision in the hands of the people. Since the no-results of France and the Netherlands, we

---

[2] The countries that had originally planned to vote were Denmark, France, the United Kingdom, Ireland, the Czech Republic, Portugal, Luxembourg, the Netherlands, and Poland. Source: The EU Information Centre of the Danish Parliament (www.eu-oplysningen.dk).

may never know whether Blair's campaigning could have resulted in a 'yes', despite the British population's general scepticism towards the EU, and the fact that the British do not have a constitution of their own.

Blair's decision to hold a referendum increased the pressure on Jacques Chirac to follow suit and call one in France. However, according to Dominique Moisi, the deciding factor was Chirac's own very low domestic popularity. Chirac mistakenly judged that the referendum would give him a victory that could lift him out of stagnation at home by increasing his personal popularity, while at the same time splitting his socialist rivals.

In Sweden, which in the past has held several referendums on EU issues – Prime Minister Göran Persson, rather like Tony Blair, must count himself one of 2005's most relieved politicians since the recent 'pause for thought' declared at the June summit in Luxembourg. Persson has persistently fought against a popular vote on the constitutional treaty on the basis that as it is so complicated it is not suitable for debate and agreement by referendum. This is a view he shares with Václav Havel. It is also a view that goes hand in hand with Persson's domestic political interests. He faces a general election in the autumn of 2006 and will have to deal with the traditional in-fighting amongst the Social Democrats regarding EU issues, as well as historically bad opinion polls. The last thing Persson would have wanted was to pioneer a yes-campaign and risk a repeat of the defeat on the adoption of the euro, which he suffered a few years ago.

In the Czech Republic, the domestic political situation is so deadlocked that no agreement can be reached as to whether to approve the constitutional treaty. Until the votes in France and the Netherlands brought a halt to the approval process – with the exception of the symbolic vote in Luxembourg – the government was leaning towards a referendum. The country was in the unusual situation whereby it looked as though it would be easier to win a referendum than get sufficient support from parliament.

However, this picture of short-sighted domestic political questions bearing upon decisions as to how to ratify the Constitution is not reflected in all the chapters of the book. In Germany, the domestic constitution does not allow for an open plebiscite, whilst in Denmark and Ireland referendums are an institution that no politician with career ambitions would dare to question. At the other end of the spectrum, we find Hungary, a country without any particular EU opposition at either a popular or a parliamentary level. Here, the parliament's approval of the constitutional treaty passed unnoticed, and without even the suggestion that a referendum might have been an option.

In Spain, Portugal and Poland, where the populations are amongst the most EU friendly, the picture is different again. Here the decisions to hold referenda were a reflection of the desire to engage the populations, whilst also sending a signal to the rest of the world. In Spain, for instance, there was no doubt that the result would be 'yes', which is why José Zapatero's government leapt at the chance to let the Spanish lead the way with the first popular mandate to the constitutional treaty. Spain would score points for pioneering, whilst at the same time sending a positive signal to the less enthusiastic French.

In both Finland and Austria, the prime ministers have had major parliamentary support and have decided not to hold referendums. The Finish prime minister, Matti Vahanen, did not believe that the treaty contained changes that were comprehensive enough to warrant a referendum. Therefore, he did not wish to run even the smallest risk of a 'no'. The argument that the constitutional treaty did not contain definitive innovations was repeated in Austria. There the majority of parties did not wish to discuss the constitutional treaty, nor give the EU sceptical population a chance to voice their opinion.

The leading parties of Italy agreed not to hold a referendum. The Italians were heavily involved in the creation of the constitutional treaty: the treaty was signed in Rome under Italian chairmanship. Despite the fact that the Italians and their politicians are usually critical of the EU, it was important for the leading parties to point out that Italy could be counted on to partake in major decisions. The population's very limited interest in EU politics meant that a controversial decision was never hinted at. During the final votes on the treaty, doubters and opponents in the parliamentary chambers accounted for less than 8%.

The Dutch decision to hold a referendum is perhaps the most surprising: eighty-five percent of the seats in the Tweede Kamer are held by EU supporters, and their last referendum was held in 1797. The closeness of the vote transpired because the EU sceptics received support from EU supporters in several of the established yes-parties. They were hoping that a referendum would engage the Dutch in European integration in general, and specifically in the constitutional treaty. Furthermore, the government's judicial body pointed out that it would be very difficult to approve the treaty without a referendum.

So there is no common reason behind the use a referendum as a democratic tool in the process towards a final acceptance or rejection of the treaty. However, again and again, domestic political considerations have played their part. Finland differs in that their prime minister did not wish to run the risk of jeopardising a yes-vote. As with Sweden, considerations were supplied by internal party-political debates. Indeed, current reasons for opting for referendums in these countries are the same as they have always been. In Denmark, referendums were only really introduced in the early 1970s, when Jens Otto Krag, the then prime minister, wished to hold a referendum on Danish acceptance into the EC to avoid a gruelling internal debate between supporters and opponents in the Social Democratic Party. Krag got his 'yes', but did not escape the debate and the no-side of the party remained. Today, all of the Danish parties in favour of the Constitution nevertheless contain elements which are opposed to it, this despite the increasing overall dominance of the yes-camp. The same is true in the rest of Europe, as will become apparent: there is generally good support for the treaty, but when the populations hit the ballots, the yes-politicians lose their grip. This problem is not unique to Danish supporters of the treaty, it is common throughout Europe.

Sovereignty, bureaucracy and open borders

If anyone has concerns that the national identity is being eroded after almost 50 years of political and financial integration in Europe, the 15 chapters of this book will ease them. Support for the nation state is thriving. Voters are prepared to vote 'no' to Europe in order to give out a domestic political message and steady the national course.

Those responsible for drafting the new Constitution were correct in restating the EU's new motto, and thereby clarifying that the prioritised goal is now an EU displaying "unity in diversity". Gone is the Treaty of Rome's objective of "an ever closer union".

When reading the 15 submissions, it is easy to see that the new motto is more in keeping with people's sentiments. The national sense of identity is very strong. No population of any country perceives itself as first and foremost European and then say, Swedish, Czech, Dutch or French. The closest we get to a population who almost prefer the EU to their own nation state is the Spanish. This may have more to do with their mistrust of their own politicians and recent memories of dictatorship than with a love for the EU.

Furthermore, the people tolerate and understand the necessity of increased integration – or to put it another way, they tolerate the EU gradually interfering in more areas. However, this development has not been actively sought by the people.

The fact is that we have hundreds of years of history, which, although often shared, has nonetheless shaped and defined the 25 Member States in different ways. Each country is characterised by knowledge of and pride in its victories, and consciousness of its defeats.

On the one hand, there is Ireland's history and background, as a country on the periphery of Europe, a country which did not endure the Second World War, whilst on the other is Poland's lengthy tale of woe, repeated humiliation, occupations, assurances, persecutions and eventual severance from the Soviet Union. But then again, those differences are not all that great after all. Both nations were oppressed for years and manipulated by larger neighbours. This engenders a national consciousness which, seen in the right light, can be expressed as defiance from the point of view of someone saying 'yes', but patriotism – and an understandable protectiveness towards often hard-won sovereignty and democracy – from the point of view of someone saying 'no'.

There is also a further gulf between the historical dictatorships of both Portugal and Spain, with their experiences of growth within the EU and the protection this has provided from home-grown politicians, and the self-confident belief of the Scandinavian countries, all too aware of their own accomplishments.

Each country is defined by its own history. On the one hand, this ties them to the EU, but on the other it defines their character as an independent state, which is capable of experiencing conflict with the coalition as a whole. France stubbornly holds on to ideas of past glory and its role as a founding member of the EU, and Britain continues to be permanently suspicious of anything continental. There is also a big difference between the homogenous society of Austria and the multiculturalism of the Netherlands, not to mention the obvious desires of the Czech Republic and Hungary to form strong ties to the West. An appreciation of these differences is crucial to our attempt to understand the various nations' relationships to the EU.

Given the varied democratic traditions and the great national differences, it is no surprise that the treaty may seem different to each country. The biggest contrast lies perhaps between the representations of Tony Blair and Jacques Chirac. Blair has been keen to emphasise that there was hardly anything new in the treaty and that the issue at stake was the reining in of the influence of the Union. Diametrically opposite was Jacques Chirac, advocating as he did a forceful and strong future Union. However, there are some common themes and alliances that recur. Amongst them are the themes of sovereignty, the interplay between welfare, enlargement and open borders, as well as centralisation, bureaucracy and a tendency to apply rules to the letter. As the chapters show, there is an obvious connection between the way in which the national debates have played out, and the individual countries' relative size, wealth and original reasons for wanting to join.

The necessary characteristic of the European collaboration – that EU law is sometimes superior to national legislation, and that a country can be vetoed and forced to implement a law – has always been a controversial cornerstone of the EU project. It has been a frequent argument of EU opponents that 'others' make all the decisions, and that it would be preferable either to stand alone, or to at least be involved in a less binding collaboration. The 15 chapters of this book show that this argument resounds with the smallest countries of the Union. Objectively seen, the smaller countries are less influential in the EU, whilst they have repeatedly been faced with defending their independence against their larger neighbour states. During its 1,000 years of history, Hungary has only existed for short periods as an independent country and, similar to other countries in the region, it has a bad relationship with the term 'integration'. When viewed from this perspective, it is perhaps unsurprising that the issue of sovereignty is a sensitive one for countries such as Denmark, Ireland, Portugal, the Czech Republic, Hungary and Austria. However, it is noteworthy that in an opinion poll in 2000, the Portuguese people pointed to the reliance of smaller countries on their larger counterparts as the EU's greatest drawback.

Sweden makes an interesting exception amongst the smaller countries, proving that the self-perception of a nation is inextricably linked to its historical circumstances. Despite the fact that Sweden's 9 million inhabitants give rise to the ratio of one Swede per 51 EU inhabitants, the Swedes still believe themselves to be a major nation. Sweden is the largest country in Scandinavia and has been accustomed to holding sway over its neighbours, at times in the role of occupier. As a result, the Swedes are not plagued by worries over losing influence, but rather wonder why the remaining countries do not emulate the Swedish model.

The Dutch and French rejections are the most recent reminders that the conjoined policies of a strong welfare state, open borders and (future) enlargements of the Union to include new and poorer countries are not uncontroversial. Such controversy is especially prevalent among the older wealthy countries with high welfare contributions. In the coming years, this matter may become yet more explosive among these countries, which, until the latest enlargement, received most aid from the EU, as well as from among the Union's newest and poorest members.[3]

---

[3] The latest opinion polls measuring EU inhabitants' general views on enlargement show that 50% of the inhabitants are supporters of new enlargements, 38% are against them and 12% are unsure. These average figures cover large national differences, which support the impressions gained from the chapters of the book that there is most support amongst the Union's most recent members as well as in Southern Europe. There is much less enthusiasm amongst the populations of the old EU countries with well-developed welfare states. Support for further enlargement in the various countries is as follows: Slovenia 79%, Poland 76%, Slovakia 73%, Cyprus 70%, Lithuania 69%, the Czech Republic 66%, Hungary 66%, Latvia 64%, Malta 63%, Greece 60%, Italy 59%, Spain 56%, Portugal 56%, Estonia 56%, Ireland 52%, Sweden 51%, Belgium 50%, Denmark 48%, the United Kingdom 48%, Germany 33%,

In the wealthy countries with high welfare contributions, the poorer sections of the populations are concerned about open borders and future enlargements. They fear that this will put a strain on their national welfare benefits. These concerns do not only afflict those workers on the lowest incomes or people on social benefits. For example, one poll shows that 76% of Austrians are worried about the influx of workers from the Eastern Member States. Wolfgang Bohm goes so far as to describe the Austrians as a people characterised by fear. They fear that their jobs will disappear and that the open borders will result in an increase in crime. This fear may seem paradoxical. The Vienna Institute for Comparative International Finances has concluded that the opening up of the Eastern markets has been hugely beneficial for Austria. Sixty thousand new jobs have been created in the last ten years, and although the open borders have made it easier for criminals to operate throughout Europe, it appears that only a minority of citizens in Austria have been personally affected.

The debate about the constitutional treaty in the Netherlands is the latest example of how decisive these concerns have become for voters in their opinion on further integration within the EU. Other issues include the possible future admission of Turkey, dissatisfaction with the speed of enlargement and the price paid for inclusion of the Eastern European countries. The debate has been shaped by fears in France of 'the Polish plumber', and a lack of reassurance that the French social model rather than the British liberal model would prevail. Despite the fact that the question of Turkey's possible inclusion was overshadowed by the more current agenda on migrating workers from the new EU countries, and bearing in mind high French unemployment, Turkey is nevertheless a smouldering issue which is likely to be rekindled at some point in the future.[4]

The problem also shows up in Denmark, where during elections we repeatedly return to the question of how to hold on to "well-earned rights" – such as our pension, early retirement allowance and free hospitals – in an EU with freedom of movement for labourers and increasing harmonisation. Suspicion alone can knock the wind out of even the best-organised yes-campaign.

Luxembourg 33%, France 32%, Austria 31%, the Netherlands 45%, Finland 45%. Source: The EU-Commission: Standard Barometer 63, July 2005.

[4] The latest opinion poll from the EU Committee underlines a great scepticism towards the admission of Turkey. When questioned whether they would support a future admission of Turkey, only 35% of the EU population were in favour of membership, 52% were against and 13% were unsure. Turkey is the least popular possible member of the study. In comparison, 78% support Norwegian membership, 52% Croatian membership and 45% Ukrainian membership. Source: The EU-Commission: Standard Barometer 63, July 2005.

In the countries that formerly belonged to the poorer group of European Member States (which in this book are represented by Portugal, Spain and, partly, Italy), the concerns are not over the potential undermining of welfare contributions, but rather that the initially substantial EU contributions, from which they benefit, will decrease dramatically once funds are redirected to new and poorer Member States. However, it is noteworthy that the populations in Spain and Portugal– insofar as they take an interest in the EU at all – have been willing to support a process that would inevitably result in less aid from the Union. It is also of interest that the issue of Turkey – despite the general scepticism – never became a campaigning issue in the Spanish referendum. Generally speaking, referendums have a tendency to change the political agenda and introduce issues such as enlargement. Take, for example, the Danish EU opponents, the June-movement, whose campaign slogan was "The EU welcomes 40 million Poles!"

Finally, all the new Eastern European members of the Union have high hopes for the collaboration, though the chapter on the Czech Republic shows clearly how quickly such hopes can turn to disappointment and scepticism towards the EU. This is not a recent tendency, and there are well-known explanations as to why such frustrations occur: people's initial enthusiasm is based on sky-high expectations and promises of financial growth so colossal that they are, of course, impossible to fulfil.

Politicians easily lapse into economic rather than political discussions, and only in those countries where the population is able to raise itself above the over-bidding of the politicians, as for instance in Poland, do we see more enthusiasm for the EU amongst ordinary people than among politicians. Following drastic remedies and brutal reform, and with the prospect of many years before the country is on a level with the 'old' EU countries, the chapter on Poland describes a people who – to a greater degree than the politicians – have long-term goals in mind and see the EU as a peacekeeper and stabiliser.

In his article, Tøger Seidenfaden points out that the EU is often described by its Danish opponents as synonymous with centralisation and bureaucracy. This picture, which in its ugliest form is about gluttony and being a stickler for the rules, can be found in several of the book's 15 chapters. The EU's image was tarnished when it emerged that the traditional method of making goulash, the Czech national dish, which involves leaving the stew to stand for several days to improve its flavour, had been banned due to the EU's tough hygiene policy. In Italy, the former finance minister and vice president in the Berlusconi government, Guilio Tremonti, has made a political issue out of highlighting the EU's pedantry for the rules in even the smallest of cases, right down to the size of bananas and onion boxes.

Despite these examples, it is worth noting that the subject does not take up much space in the book. The people and politicians know how to sneer at the EU for its centralisation, bureaucracy and high wages, but when it comes to a general attitude to the EU, the concerns are over sovereignty, influence, open borders and so on. That these former issues lack impact in the majority of EU countries can possibly be explained by remembering that many EU populations are accustomed to bureaucracy. Furthermore, the national administrations of many Member States can hardly criticise the EU on subjects such as openness and intrusion into people's daily lives. The issue's relatively low billing on the political agenda does not mean that it is irrelevant. Persistent wear and tear on an institution's image does carry a risk, and there are all sorts of good reasons to continue working towards reforming the EU's administration. However, the chapters of this book underline that one cannot rely simply on a reformation of the EU institutions (increased efficiency, more openness and simpler decision-making) as a means to change the people's support of the Union.

In Denmark, the yes-campaigns start well but consistently lose ground and cannot sustain the ratings. The chapters in this book show that this is not a uniquely Danish phenomenon. The yes-campaigns often proceed without a clear focal point and the lack of clear and recurring yes-arguments across the countries is remarkable. In several countries, the support from the political elite is hesitant, half-hearted and almost non-existent. Among these politicians, this lack of positive engagement is increasingly turning into shrill warnings about the dangers of saying 'no', whilst the 'no' side's position is gradually strengthened. When a 'no' is evident, politicians change their style again. Suddenly they understand and respect public concerns over increased integration.

This somewhat caricatured pattern could be seen in the Netherlands, where almost a third of the opponents pointed towards the government's scare tactics as their reason for voting 'no'. This is also recognisable from previously unsuccessful yes-campaigns; for instance, the Danish referendum on the Maastricht Treaty and the Swedish vote on the euro. It is easy to jibe at the yes-politicians for their behaviour, but selling a 'yes' is not easy. The basis for such campaigns is problematic, since in the periods between possible referendums there is hardly any talk about the EU in the national media. When politicians start mentioning the EU it is usually as a scapegoat. A classic example from Denmark is the directive concerning the bend on cucumbers, for which the EU was roundly castigated by all politicians until it was discovered that the directive had been requested by the Danish. The directive was meant to ensure quality and low prices for the consumers! With such stories in the back of our minds, it is no wonder that it can be hard to teach the population to love the EU in the few weeks leading up to an election. After all, in the periods between elections the EU is blamed for all that is bad, whilst the national politicians are quick to take credit for any of the Union's successes.

The relationship is exacerbated when – as in the case of the constitutional treaty – it is a case of selling a proposed compromise aimed at uniting 25 countries and even more than 25 party-political trends. During the period in which the treaty was finally negotiated, we saw such diverse parties in power as Jörg Haider's extreme right in Austria, the Swedish Social Democrats, French conservatives, and the feet-dragging British New Labour.

During the process, the various countries' leaders and other leading politicians have identified a number of single issues as being decisive and, from this position, each has had to make concessions in order to reach a compromise. Each country has been left with something functional, better than the previous treaty but not optimal. Significantly, no one has perceived himself as victorious when debating which model to follow in the battle between the Anglo-Saxon neo-liberal market model, and the French/German/North European social model.

The aim was to sell a compromise of which no Member State could claim 100% ownership, and this in the face of national populations hardly interested in the EU itself, let alone the precise terms of the proposed constitution. As Teresa de Sousa says is the case in Portugal, the "indifference party" is strongest in most of the Member States.

It is characteristic that the voters have used the constitutional treaty to express their opinion on leading politicians, or on issues that can be broadly linked to the EU. The chapters in this book show that it was bad luck for the constitutional treaty that several of the governments needing to convince their people of its virtues were themselves deeply unpopular. Dutch researchers have questioned whether it is at all possible for an unpopular government to win an EU election, particularly at a time of financial depression and faced with a population wary of immigrants. Spain was an exception, and Andrés Ortega highlights the recent change in government as one of the Spaniards' reasons for accepting their politicians' endorsement of the treaty.

France

When Jacques Chirac called the referendum on the constitutional treaty, he thought he was on to a winner. However, Chirac underestimated both his own unpopularity and the public's dissatisfaction with past enlargements. The French fear that their country will lose influence in the larger Union and there is a growing sense of insecurity with respect to the political direction of a Union that is no longer linked to prosperity but to unemployment. Europeanisation equates with globalisation for the 'no' camp. And the yes-camp failed to convince the French that the real problem was not the 'Polish plumber' but the Chinese and Indian workers. On the political arena, the protectionist tendency was encouraged by an alliance between the extreme right and extreme left.

The French Say 'No' To Enlargement, Globalisation And Chirac

by Dominique Moisi

Dominique Moisi is a senior adviser at the French Institute of International Relations. He also writes columns for The Financial Times and Le Monde.

The French and Dutch 'no' to the constitutional treaty on 29 May and 1 June 2005 may be seen by historians of the early 21st century as a symbolic turning point for Europe. A date that will enter history as surely as 9 November 1989 did. While the fall of the Berlin Wall was a much more spectacular event marking the end of the cold war, the French 'no', followed by the Dutch one, may mark the end of the post-war period: a period characterised by a sort of reverence to a European Union associated with peace, prosperity and freedom. The cause of Europe was common ground for a majority of Europeans. But for the young French and Dutch who have voted 'no' to the constitutional treaty, peace is not a marvellous conquest, it is the only situation they have known, and the high level of unemployment makes the association between the words 'Europe' and 'prosperity' at best an irony and at worst a provocation.

May 29 provided a moment for reflection and listening. What has really happened can be summarised in three words: enlargement, globalisation and

Chirac, if by including the name of the French president here one means the growing divorce between society and the political elites in France. One was expecting the ghost of the Turkish worker to weaken the yes-camp; instead it was the 'Polish plumber'. The issue of enlargement proved decisive, not a future enlargement, but those of the past. In reality, according to public opinion polls, the issue of Turkey was mentioned by only 14% of the no-camp to justify their votes. But if the Turkish issue was not responsible for the no-vote to the Constitution, the no-result may delay the Turkish candidacy becoming a full member to the European Union forever.

The French were not directly consulted on 1 May 2004 to approve the passage of Europe from 15 to 25 members. On 29 May 2005, they expressed their sense of alienation towards the New Europe. Yesterday's Europe, for France, was the pursuit of national ambition through other means, the mechanism through which one could continue a policy of glory and influence. Through the Franco-German partnership, the French could continue to perceive themselves as the head of the European family. Today, looking at the table of 25, they have lost that sense of familiarity and predominance. The European Union is acting like a mirror reflecting their growing sense of insecurity. Who are these people whose languages I do not recognise, whose faces and names are unknown to me and who tend, in diplomatic terms, to listen to Washington more than Paris?

If Europe is no longer the continuation of France, it is also because it is no longer linked to prosperity but unemployment in the popular imagination. For the no-camp, Europeanisation equates with globalisation, i.e. delocalisation. And the yes-camp has failed to convince the French that the real problem was not the Polish plumber but the Chinese and Indian workers. This strong protectionist tendency is, of course, encouraged by the unholy alliance between the extreme right and extreme left, and the lack of charisma of the majority of France's and Europe's political elites at large. There is a direct connection between the level of education and revenues and the vote. This correlation was obvious in a city like Paris who voted for the 'yes' in a proportion that was directly linked to the value of the housing market; the higher the price, the more likely the vote in favour of the Constitution. It was not only a division between the 'haves' and 'have nots', but also one between those who believed in the future and those – like the majority of farmers – who were afraid of it.

The backlash against enlargement and globalisation may have constituted inevitable trends. The 'accident' of history may have been the presence, at this critical juncture, of the man in power in France, who may well go down in history as the weakest president of the Fifth Republic. A man who could not be the right messenger for the constitutional treaty because the message was difficult to convey objectively, and because the messenger was, at best, tedious on the subject of Europe. According to recent public opinion polls, the Germans too would have said 'no' to the constitutional treaty if they had been consulted in a referendum. When representative and direct democracies give such different results, it is the very nature of democracy that is in crisis.

Why did President Chirac taken the risk of using the referendum, given the fact that he was not obliged to do so? Three factors may have proven decisive. The first one is the Gaullist tradition of referendum, the direct call on the people to decide on matters that are judged essential for the future of the nation. The second factor is Tony Blair's decision to go through with a referendum himself for his country. Jacques Chirac felt, so to speak, obliged to imitate him. But if he did so, it was essentially for a combination of domestic political calculus. Since the first ballot of the presidential elections in 2002, when he received less than 20% of the popular vote, the French president had felt he had a legitimacy problem. He was the legal president of France, and had been re-elected with a huge majority of 82% of the votes on the second ballot, crushing the candidate of the extreme right, Jean Marie Le Pen. But in 2004, he realised his popularity was very low. Why not use the issue of Europe to rebuild his legitimacy? The risks were bound to be limited. Could the French ever say 'no' to Europe? On top of it, he would expose the divisions existing within the socialist party on the European issues.

Jacques Chirac, once again, as in 1997 when he chose to dissolve the National Assembly to get a stronger majority and found himself with a socialist majority in the parliament, made the wrong choice; for himself, for France and, in this case, for Europe. One thing remains to be said. The results of the French referendum exposed the growing uneasiness of the French not only with Europe, but also more deeply with their own identity. Insecure with their performance in the world of globalisation, the French were asking themselves more fundamental questions about their essence, and their ability to preserve their model of social protection and national cohesion in an open, interdependent and increasingly dangerous and competitive world.

In this context of self-interrogation, self-doubts and deep morosity it would be dangerous to proceed as if nothing had happened, as if the ratification process could go on unimpeded. Recent opinion polls suggest that a majority of Germans would reject the constitutional treaty too if they could express their view in a referendum. Only a combination of masochism, blindness and arrogance could lead us to proceed on the ratification path. Even if the success of the 'no' is at least as much linked to domestic reasons as to a growing frustration with Europe, and even if the coalition of the extreme right and left does not constitute a coherent majority, to ignore the significance of the two no-votes would constitute the safest means to delegitimise the cause of Europe in the eyes of Europeans, and to further alienate citizens from their political elites.

To cling to old recipes, such as the evocation of the Franco-German partnership, will not do either. The raison d'être of such a self-appointed *avant-garde* would be to set a good example. But this is precisely what France and Germany have refrained from doing in many fields of European integration. Moreover, how can two sick men who refuse to fight their domestic diseases seriously believe that they will be accepted as a vanguard?

Yet if a pause is necessary, it should not be equated with immobilisation and inaction. In the meantime, four directions have to be pursued. The first one consists of saving foreign policy from electoral disaster. Europe must not be perceived by countries such as the United States, China and Russia as irrelevant, passive and totally obsessed with herself. Whatever the title it should be given – high representative, foreign minister, vice-president – the position of Javier Solana must be extricated from the political hurricane that has engulfed Europe. If Europe needs to 'pause' inside, it must demonstrate some political will to the outside world. Such a requirement can be understood by a majority of Europeans and will not be perceived as a transgression of the diffident vote of the majority of French and Dutch citizens.

The second and even more fundamental field for action concerns economic and social reforms. Germany, France and some other countries have not done enough in terms of the labour market, welfare state and budget reforms. The static and relatively rigid continental social model cannot be pursued anymore. Only if this homework is done, might we be able to overcome the European paralysis. To quote Minister of Interior Nicolas Sarkozy, it is necessary to "give back reality to the social model". And the alternatives to pure market-dictated economies exist more in Nordic Europe and the United Kingdom, than in traditional continental Europe.

Thirdly, in spite of the fact that the no-vote was in part the product of the negative reaction of many Frenchmen to past enlargement and the passage of Europe from 15 to 25 members, the cause of enlargement must be fought for with courage and determination by Europe's political elites. It must be explained that enlargement constitutes Europe's greatest political triumph and not Europe's greatest economic catastrophe. Delocalisation is not the product of 'Europeanisation' but of globalisation. It is not the Polish plumber but the Chinese and Indian workers that constitute the greatest challenge for Europe's labour force. The process of enlargement must continue and include the two countries already accepted, Bulgaria and Rumania, and in time all of the Balkans countries that can satisfy the

European Union's criteria. But we cannot proceed as if the people of Europe had not expressed themselves; as if the feelings and emotions of the majority view in two countries on the passionate identity question did not exist.

The fourth field of action is directly linked to the current budgetary process. The battle over the new budget for the EU can deepen the atmosphere of separation between the old and the new Member States (and among the old ones) or it can contribute to the improvement of the atmosphere in Europe if the principle of solidarity is clearly reaffirmed. It is essential to reach a compromise rapidly, especially between France, Germany, the United Kingdom, Italy, Poland, and Spain.

In post-war Europe, crisis situations often served as challenges and opportunities to push forward the cause of European integration. In 1954, the French National Assembly rejected the European Defence Community. In that critical situation, a group of countries concentrated on the economy in the pursuit of European integration. We can now once again transform a crisis into an opportunity, providing we manifest the will to strengthen our togetherness, to reform our economies and be ready to take our share of responsibility in world affairs.

We have been taking Europe for granted. What has been achieved through patient efforts in the last 50 years can be unravelled much more quickly. It will not be a return to the wars of the past, but surely a sliding into irrelevance. If it keeps missing appointments with history, the fate of the European Union can be that of the Republic of Venice; once a key actor in world affairs, now turned into a museum for others, more dynamic and more determined to succeed.

The Netherlands

The referendum about the constitutional treaty was the first time the Dutch population had been consulted on an EU question and the '*nee*' revealed a deep chasm between the people and the politicians. One third of the naysayers stated that the reason they had voted against the treaty was grounded in the government's scare campaign. The referendum was used to express a rising anxiety and dissatisfaction with immigration, the Netherlands' role as one of the EU's biggest financial contributors, and to voice the fear of losing sovereignty, identity and influence in the Union. The Dutch majority has no problems with a close and committed partnership, but they have no desire for further integration in an even bigger European Union.

The Constitutional Treaty As An Emergency Brake: The Dutch Get Off The Integration Train

by Syp Wynia

Syp Wynia was the Brussels-based correspondent of the Dutch daily newspaper Het Parool from 1992 to 1997 and, since then, has written on Dutch and European politics for the weekly magazine Elsevier.

On the first day of June 2005, a majority of 61.5% of the Dutch citizens said '*nee*' to the constitutional treaty of the European Union. The rejection of the European Constitution was even more overwhelming as 63.3% of the voters came to the ballot, many more than was expected. The vote was not only a blow to the ratification process of the 25 Member States of the European Union, but also a blow to the Dutch political establishment that had rallied for a '*ja*' to the Constitution. Only the small, left-wing liberal party, D66, had the backing of a majority of its voters in favour of the Constitution. All other '*ja*' parties, including the CDA of Prime Minister Jan Peter Balkenende (52%), his mainstream-liberal coalition partner of the VVD (62%) and the PvdA (Labour opposition, 62%) had to face the fact that a majority of their voters voted against the European Constitution in the elections of January 2003. The referendum gave a boost to the no-campaigners of the ultra left Socialist Party, the small protestant ChristenUnie and the new right-wing political entrepreneur, Geert Wilders.

Large majorities of their followers indeed voted 'no' and these parties also rose in polls in the aftermath of the referendum.

After the referendum, the Dutch government announced a research project on the reasons why the Dutch voted as they did. At the same time, private research institutions signalled that the fact that the Dutch are the biggest net payers in the European Union played a prominent role in the way they voted, in combination with attitudes against the future membership of Turkey, dissatisfaction with the euro and losing influence and identity in Europe. A relatively small group (11 %) openly admitted that their negative feelings towards the current Dutch government had played a decisive role.

Only the richest suburban areas in the Netherlands voted in favour of the European Constitution. Traditional, orthodox, protestant areas like fishermen's communities were among the most negative on the Constitution. In general, the highest earners and the best educated tended to be in favour, the lower sociological classes tended against. Women were more against than men, the elder voters more in favour than the middle-aged, and the Christian-religious were generally more in favour than non-believers. Also the youngest group, those less than 25, showed a more than average support for the Constitution. Almost a third of the voters said that the government-led campaign for them had worked counter-productively: towards a 'no'.

It was the first time ever that the citizens of the Kingdom of the Netherlands, founded in 1813, had the opportunity to give their opinion in a referendum on any item. Only once, under semi-French rule in 1797, had there been a referendum; then it was also on a constitution, one that would have transformed the former Dutch Republic, a confederacy with sovereign provinces, into a central state. In the same year, the Dutch overwhelmingly rejected this centralising project. But, after a coup d'état, the new constitution, called 'the Thick Book' as it had 918 articles, was rewritten and accepted the following year. But in recent times there has never been a national referendum, and so neither national politicians nor national officials had any experience with plebiscites. This would appear to be a serious handicap for the '*ja*' campaigners. However, it appeared to be not the only handicap.

But how did the Dutch get their referendum? The first suggestions to hold a referendum on the European integration arose in June 2002. It was only weeks after the national elections of 15 May 2002, which had been a big success for the young party of Pim Fortuyn, the new maverick politician who had been assassinated nine days earlier. The parliamentary group of the late Fortuyn, which supported the first centre-right Balkenende government formed after the elections, asked for a referendum on the EU's enlargement of the ten Eastern and Central European and Mediterranean countries that would be negotiated later that year. After some weeks, the Lijst Pim Fortuyn (LPF) took back this proposal as part of the governing agreement with the Christian democrats of the CDA and the liberals of the VVD. But the rise of Fortuyn, who was sceptical on the many aspects of the European integration, made Dutch politicians less secure about following mainstream policies in the European Union without consulting the general public.

The possibility of a referendum returned to the Dutch political agenda, and again on a European topic: the Constitution. In the weeks before the European Summit near Thessaloniki, on 19-20 June 2003 where the results of the Convention on the Constitution would be presented, there was a debate in the Tweede Kamer, the Dutch House of Commons, during which there appeared to be a small majority for a national referendum on the future Constitution. The initiative was partly from Frans Timmermans, a Labour member of parliament who had been a member of the Convention. He thought a referendum would be a good instrument to get the Dutch people involved with the new Constitution and with European integration in general. He convinced his party, who were in opposition, and was also supported by two other small pro-Constitution political parties: GroenLinks (Green-Left, opposition) and D66 (left-wing liberals, and a junior partner in the second Balkenende government, now without the LPF that had shrunk after new elections in January 2003).

A decisive role was played by Jozias van Aartsen, the former minister of foreign affairs, who was the new leader of the VVD party, which was once more a partner in the new Balkenende government. In the early days of September 2003, Van Aartsen convinced his parliamentary group that a referendum on the Constitution should be supported. So the referendum was an initiative of parties that both opposed and supported the government. The CDA, the party of Prime Minister Jan Peter Balkenende, was not in favour but had to accept the parliamentary majority on the referendum. Advice from the main legal advisory board of the government, the Raad van State, was crucial. This council wrote that to change the national Constitution, the Grondwet, a difficult parliamentary routing was needed. A two-thirds majority in both Houses of Parliament would be necessary, and that the ratification of the European Constitution with a simple majority in both Houses of Parliament was probably too easy. Therefore, the Council concluded, a referendum on the European Constitution would be a possibility to find a more generous, public, democratic backing for this far-reaching treaty.

Finally, on 25 January 2005, the Dutch Senate, the Eerste Kamer, also accepted the legislation needed to hold this referendum. Formally, the referendum would be advice from the Dutch citizens for the Tweede Kamer.

Some parties immediately said that the outcome of the referendum would be binding for them. The PvdA (Labour Party) wanted a turnout of at least 30% of voters in order to respect the outcome. Prime Minister Balkenende's CDA, which opposed the referendum, would nevertheless accept the outcome with at least 30% of the population voting and a result of 60% (later this was changed to 55%). The VVD hesitated until the end of May 2005, but then the party of Van Aartsen and Finance Minister Gerrit Zalm announced they would accept any result.

All the main political parties, with a total of 85% of the seats in the Tweede Kamer, supported the European Constitution. And, of course, so did the government. Prime Minister Balkenende was one of the signatories at the session in Rome, on 29 October 2004. The support of the coalition party VVD for the Constitution had not always been clear, however. It was only after the European Council in Brussels, on 18 June 2004, when the Constitution was finalised, that the parliamentary group of the VVD made the change to 'yes'. This was following the prime minister, Mr. Balkenende, reaching agreement on the paragraph in the Constitution that qualified majority voting on the European seven-year budget would only be possible after the Dutch were satisfied on the structure of their negative net payer's position. The prime minister also got some wording included on the role of the European Commission and the European Court on the Stability and Growth pact for euro-zone countries.

So the coalition parties, the CDA, VVD and D66 supported the Constitution, as did the PvdA and the Greens in the opposition. The '*nee*' camp had only 15% of the seats in the Tweede Kamer: the Socialist Party and the Lijst Pim Fortuyn, two small protestant parties and the former VVD politician, Geert Wilders. This right-wing liberal left the VVD in the early days of September 2004 after problems with Jozias van Aartsen, especially on the future EU membership of Turkey, which he principally opposed. Wilders, who then started his own party, grew very popular in the polls after 2 November 2004, when an Islamist of Moroccan descent murdered the Dutch writer and filmmaker, Theo van Gogh. Wilders, just like his former parliamentary colleague, Ayaan Hirsi Ali (who is from Somalia and made the film 'Submission' with Van Gogh) had to go into hiding after threatening letters where found on the body of Van Gogh. Jan Marijnissen, the leader of the Socialist Party and Geert Wilders were the main politicians of the no-campaign. They were later accompanied by a respected young politician, André Rouvoet, of the small protestant ChristenUnie and the European specialist of Marijnissen's party, Harry van Bommel.

The Dutch government, not experienced with referendums, had planned to concentrate on the campaign during the last two weeks of May. Apparently this decision had to do with the recent election experience, especially the national elections of January 2003, which were decided in a highly television-dominated battle of only two weeks. The Dutch debate on the Constitution was, until the middle of April 2005, somewhat overshadowed by the French run-up to their referendum that was being held only three days before the Dutch one. Until then, the Dutch media were very quiet on the Constitution and the Dutch referendum. The silence was broken by the weekly magazine, *Elsevier*, which in the edition of 16 April advised the readers to vote 'no'. "Why NO is better than yes", the cover said. A key argument of the magazine was that the Constitution facilitates the transfer of national powers on migration to Brussels, and creates more easy access to welfare in the Netherlands for citizens of Member States and third-country nationals that are legalised in other Member States of the enlarging European Union. The Netherlands have an experience of non-western immigrants and their descendants (Turks, Moroccans, former asylum seekers and others), who already make up 10% of the population and this number is growing. These people are three to five times more likely to be unemployed and dependent on welfare, social benefits and other state arrangements. *Elsevier* was the only publication that advised 'no' but in other newspapers, independent columnists started to write about their doubts on whether the Constitution – partly in relation to the enlarging EU – was a good thing for the Netherlands and the European Union in general.

So on Friday, 15 April, Mr Balkenende's government somewhat hastily started their campaign, firstly in a news programme on public television that only showed Constitution supporters. Over the next few days, Secretary of Justice Piet Hein Donner suggested that a rejection of the Constitution could lead to war in Europe and used the comparison with former Yugoslavia in the Nineties. Ben Bot, secretary of foreign affairs, said that the EU would be unmanageable without the Constitution. This was the central tone in the first weeks of the government's campaign: dark scenario's for the Netherlands and for Europe without a Dutch 'yes'. This was apparently counterproductive. The Dutch reacted negatively to the warnings of the already deeply unpopular government that had the support of less than 20% of the people and also because the Dutch economy, after five years of high-growth figures at the end of the 1990s, had deteriorated for five years now and was a bad performer, even in the stagnating euro zone as a whole. Researchers at Amsterdam University predicted that it would be almost impossible for a European government in a country with economic pessimism and worries about migration to win a referendum on a European issue, if that government was not popular itself.

In the middle of 2004, there was still a majority in favour of the Constitution. At the end of January 2005, when the definitive decision on the referendum was taken, about half of those who had decided to vote were against, and the other half was in favour. But after the first sombre warnings of the yes-politicians, the yes-campaign lost ground. On 23 April, the pollster Maurice de Hond saw a small majority of 52% against the Constitution from the people who had decided they would vote. At the time however, only 32% of the Dutch planned to vote.

In the following weeks, members of the government went on with rallying against the 'no'; more than that, they were rallying in favour of a 'yes'. Prime Minister Jan Peter Balkenende called the no-voters "negative and naive", warned that other EU countries would punish the Netherlands for a 'no', and used – misused, as many people said – the national days of commemoration at the beginning of May and the visit of US President George W. Bush to an American war cemetery near the Dutch village of Margraten for campaigning on the 'yes'. The prime minister also used earlier visits to Auschwitz and the memory site, Yad Vashem, in Israel as a reason to say 'yes' to the Constitution, and suggested that the Dutch Queen Beatrix and Crown Prince Willem Alexander were in favour of the Constitution.

Immigration Minister Rita Verdonk suggested that without the Constitution many more immigrants would come to the Netherlands. Ben Bot now warned against an economical crisis. Similarly, the minister of Economical Affairs, Laurens Jan Brinkhorst, stated on 10 May: "In the long run, the light goes out and the country will be closed down." All these statements worked in favour of the no-campaign, which was much less visible in the media. The yes-majority had a lot of problems explaining the advantages of the Constitution and their intimidating tone irritated a lot of the Dutch.

On 21 May, the pollster Maurice de Hond said that 43% of the Dutch planned to vote and that 60% of them would vote against the Constitution. He concluded that quite a lot of people chose to vote 'no' because of the fuss around the introduction of the euro. On 30 April, Dutch newspapers had cited a high-ranking official of the Dutch Central Bank, who said that the Dutch guilder had been "too cheap" when it went into the euro in 1998. This gave new rise to the distrust of many Dutch citizens for the European currency. They blamed the euro, introduced in 2002, for their shrinking budgets. The fact that Germany and France in previous years did not follow the budget rules of the Stability Pact – also a reason for worries for the government – made the image of the euro even worse and fed distrust on European treaties like the Constitution.

Another main theme was the future EU enlargement to include Turkey – left off the referendum agenda by the government – and a very unpopular theme in the Netherlands where the Turkish population is the largest immigrant-group. The Turkey-issue grew even more unpopular after the assassination of Theo van Gogh by a Muslim terrorist. Other less prominent items were animal rights in the EU Constitution and the future of the Dutch 'coffee shops' (where cannabis is sold semi-legally) in a European Union with more federalised criminal legislation. The fact that the Dutch government was already deeply unpopular was also, directly or indirectly, a factor for the Dutch to say 'no'. After a majority of the French said 'no' on 29 May, the tendency to say 'no' in the Netherlands increased.

Immediately after the exit polls on the evening of 1 June showed the clear 'no', the Dutch government and also the other politicians that had supported the European Constitution made U-turns. Prime Minister Balkenende said he was very disappointed, but praised the debate and repeated that neither he nor the rest of the government saw the results of the referendum as a reason to leave. "We understand the worries of the Dutch," the prime minister said. "About the loss of sovereignty. About the pace of change without the people feeling that they are involved. About our financial contribution. Europe should consider this as well." Secretary of the Treasury Gerrit Zalm immediately used the no-vote for his long-time struggle to get the Dutch financial net contribution more in balance with other EU countries, now in the run-up to the European Council of 16-17 June, where the financial perspectives were on the agenda.

The next day the government withdrew the proposal to the parliament to accept the European Treaty. During the parliamentary debate on the vote, even the yes-campaigners, like Labour leader Wouter Bos, said they were "proud" on having had the referendum. The new consensus in Dutch politics seemed to imply there should be a rethinking on Dutch European politics and that, after such a long time without serious political debate on European integration, the general public should be involved in any new step. Some politicians also saw the (sometimes lukewarm) support of established Dutch organisations like trade unions and employers as a sign that these organisations were probably also out of touch with their own members and the rest of society. In this respect, the referendum supported earlier doubts on the traditional Dutch consensus model. The referendum also gave a new boost to discussions on the functioning of the Dutch democracy, a discussion that has been going of for four decades but has never resulted in a new system. Contrasting with the international image of a democratic and transparent country, Dutch citizens don't have the right to vote for the head of state, the head of government, the head of the region, or the head of the local administration. After local, regional and also national elections, it is usually a surprise to discover which coalition will get into power. As members of parliament don't have their own constituency, the direct link between voters and representatives is usually weak. This system has the risk of creating a structural gap between the general public and the public class, as this first referendum in the history of the Kingdom of the Netherlands has also signalled. Partly as a fall-out of the referendum, the government is

preparing proposals about a renewal of the democratic system, possibly with
more referendums and possibly with the creation of direct constituency links
between voters and their representative. Some parties, also, surprisingly, the
usually conservative VVD, are now in favour of a directly elected prime
minister.

The result of the Dutch referendum has, at least partly, to be seen against the
background of a high volatility in election results in the past 11 years. The
results of 1994 (huge losses for the coalition parties, CDA and PvdA), 2002
(a comeback for the CDA, big losses for the other established parties and the
rise of the Fortuyn-party), and 2003 (a comeback for the PvdA, a big loss
for the Fortuyn-politicians) are among the most volatile in recent European
history. The main political parties and their leaders have lost the stable
backing of their voters. In the past 40 years, Dutch society has changed quite
dramatically, from an internationally orientated but traditional society with
strong binding features and a very limited economical role for women, to a
socially and culturally liberal country with a highly developed welfare
system, upon which a growing part of the population is dependent.
Traditional institutions (churches, political parties, trade unions) have lost
their grip on society. This erosion of cohesion grew even further as a result
of the influx of immigrants: former 'guest-workers' from Turkey and
Morocco who stayed and brought in their families, people from the former
Dutch colonies like Surinam, and asylum seekers from Asia, Africa and the
Balkans. In the meantime, post-colonial and post-Holocaust sentiments
made the traditional, already strong, morally driven Dutch political class
react cautiously to talk about the negative aspects of the new Dutch society,
like the rise of crime and the high unemployment of immigrants. Frits
Bolkestein of the VVD broke this morally biased attitude of the main Dutch
politicians. He opened the official debate on migration, integration of
immigrants, and the role of Islam in 1991, but, later on, also on the Dutch
perception of the 'ever closer' European Union. After Bolkestein left Dutch
politics in 1999 to become a European commissioner, his party leaned
towards the then coalition partner, the PvdA, and lost its attraction to many
new voters, and so created an electoral gap that was used by Pim Fortuyn,
who also attracted earlier non-voters and supporters of other political
parties. Geert Wilders, the now new kid on the block seems to attract a less
wide public, but is still a problem for the VVD that he left. In general,
however, there is no sign that voter volatility and – as it is sometimes
wrongly referred – populism will end after the recent elections and the
Dutch referendum on the European Constitution. A better performance of
the Dutch economy, however, would possibly help the current and future
governments to regain trust.

In this referendum, it became clear that also the official 'correct' consensus
in the Dutch political class on the European integration was broken. For

outsiders this could be a surprise, but for insiders it was not. The Dutch history on post-war European integration has in fact always contained some in-built contradictions. The Netherlands are one of the founding countries of post-war European integration. In 1948, The Hague hosted the European Congress, where the European Council was founded. In 1950, the Netherlands was one of the six countries that supported the Schuman plan that resulted in the European Community for Coal and Steel. The Dutch government supported the Pleven plan for a European Defence Community, which resulted in the French Assembly in 1954, but was in favour of an intergovernmental model for the Community because it wanted to keep the door open for defence cooperation with the UK. The Netherlands kept this position somehow until recently: European cooperation should be firstly economical cooperation. The Dutch minister, Jan Willem Beyen, was one of the writers of the Benelux memorandum that formed the basis of the European Economic Community and the Treaty of Rome, signed in 1957. In the Sixties, the Dutch minister of foreign affairs, Joseph Luns, rivalled with the French president, Charles de Gaulle, and pleaded for British membership, that – after the resignation of De Gaulle – was accorded in 1969 at The Hague Summit. New treaties were completed under Dutch presidencies: Maastricht, 1991 and Amsterdam, 1997.

So, the official Dutch policy was always pro-European, but it especially favoured the Internal Market and was sceptical of French-German domination, especially on Foreign and Defence policies. The main parties were somewhat split: some politicians where more Atlanticist, some in favour of speeding up European integration and others were more generally internationalist and in favour of the United Nations. International policy and especially the European integration were seldom a theme in the broader public debate, however. Europe was no topic during election campaigns. The Dutch citizens had, generally, a positive attitude towards European integration: they felt that it was good for the economy, but they were also quite indifferent on this theme.

From 1991 onwards, scepticism on European integration was introduced in the Dutch political debate. Frits Bolkestein, the VVD leader, was the first main politician that was openly sceptical on the 'ever closer union' and made this public after the Danish rejection of the Maastricht Treaty in 1992. The official Dutch line was, for the first time in 1994, critical on the costs and the worldwide effects of the European agricultural policies, and also on the way European structural funds were distributed from rich countries to other rich countries. Bolkestein and his party were disparaging on the Dutch net payer's position, a critical position that was part of the 1998 coalition deal of the second Kok cabinet. Bolkestein also was openly disapproving on the Italian membership of the euro-zone.

The Dutch public got the message and was also disappointed after the introduction of the euro in 2002, when the economy soared and many people had the feeling that it was at least partly due to the euro. The VVD, now supported by the political group of the late Pim Fortuyn, was negative on a 'Big Bang' enlargement with ten new countries. In the background, a feeling was growing that the Netherlands, still proud of its history as a small world power in the 17th century and a colonial power until the 1940s, was getting smaller and less influential in the widening European construction. So, from 1991 onwards, Dutch politicians followed by the Dutch public grew more sceptical on European integration. A general feeling of loss of national sovereignty and national identity was part of that process.

The concept of an 'ever closer' European integration, widely supported for a long time by Dutch European politics, grew weaker in the Nineties and especially in the early years of the new century. This concept receded in the days after the overwhelming 'no' of the Dutch citizens and became clear during the parliamentary debate after the referendum. The referendum showed that the majority of the Dutch are not in favour of an increased transfer of powers to a centrally organised European Union with federalist features. They don't like the fact that this European Union is enlarging fast, with the side-effect that founder nations, like the Netherlands, have less influence on their own fate. In fact, this development could have been foreseen during the Dutch elections of the European Parliament in 1994 and 1999; both showed a then surprisingly low turnout of less than a third of the electorate. In 2004, the turnout saw a rise to 39%, but researchers found that many of the new voters were protest voters (for the European dissident, Paul van Buitenen, and the Party for the Animals) who had mostly stayed away during earlier European elections.

It seems impossible for a leading Dutch politician to win future elections with a plea for further enlargement and further integration of the European Union. The Dutch parliament asked the Dutch citizens, for the first time in half a century, what they thought of the present direction of European integration. The Dutch political establishment probably did not like the answer, but they have to live up to it. The majority of the Dutch appear not to be against close cooperation, but are not in favour of more integration in a larger European Union. That was the main lesson on that first day of June 2005.

Italy

For Italy, it is important to play a leading role in the European partnership, but there are signs of an Italian paradox: a mixture of enthusiasm for Europe and pragmatic Euro-scepticism. On the one hand, there is a long and unbroken tradition in Italy for supporting European integration in the direction of federalism and, on the other, there is uncertainty about the social and economic future. There was never any doubt that the constitutional treaty would be ratified in Italy, where the naysayers' arguments always met with an unsympathetic response. Still, the ratification was not due to great public enthusiasm, since the Italians are not especially engaged with the European Union. When the constitutional treaty was signed in Rome, the Italian population's primary response had been only lukewarm enthusiasm

The Italian Paradox: Enthusiasm And Scepticism Go Hand In Hand

by Giuseppe Sarcina (translated by Margaret Stenhouse)

Giuseppe Sarcina is a Brussels-based correspondent for Corriere della Sera.

On 29 October 2004, the Italian prime minister, Silvio Berlusconi, signed the European Constitution charter with the biggest 'B' (for Berlusconi) in the history of Italian diplomatic relations. It was a kind of seal, a metaphorical expression of the Berlusconi ego, but it was also a way of declaring that Italy was present, as always. Yet for some time, that same prime minister had never missed a chance to criticise European institutions. The most recent instance took place on 19 March 2005, when the premier declared at a conference of Confindustria (the association of Italian industrialists): "Brussels is populated by hominoids – little bureaucrats who, like the Lilliputians, are only interested in tethering the giant Gulliver." (He was referring to the European economy). The image was borrowed from 'Competitive Day', the campaign launched by the Union of Associations of European Industrialists, UNICE, in Brussels on 14 November 2003. In his role as rotating president of the EU, Berlusconi took part as a special guest and carried home at the end a couple of manifestos from the fettered 'industrial Gulliver'.

All this means that there is probably no other country today like Italy where such a strange paradox exists. The government demands less Europe on the one hand, but on the other, at crucial moments, claims a leading role in the building of the EU. The same kind of attitude was repeated in the weeks following the referendums in France and Holland, and after the failure to reach agreement on the 'financial prospects' at the European Council meeting on 16 and 17 June 2005 in Brussels. The double 'no' from the Netherlands and France, and the failure of the summit, boosted the Euro-sceptic wing of the centre-right government. The attitude of the Italian ruling class towards Europe seems to be conditioned by two contrasting political-psychological forces: on the one side there is the weight of a long and continuous tradition of pro-European integration, if not to say semi-federalism, and on the other, there is the uncertainty and lack of security regarding the social and economic future of the country. These two trains of thought – two 'political souls' – develop along parallel lines, launching contradictory images and messages outside Italy. During the six-month Italian presidency (June-December 2003), Berlusconi shifted frenetically from one side to the other of this symbolic space. In July 2003, he provoked an incident in the Strasbourg Parliament, which was perhaps without precedent, by quarrelling with the Socialist MEP Martin Schulz ("you could play a supporting role as a 'kapo' in a film on nazism"). But, at the same time, the premier urged the other heads of state and government to sign the constitutional treaty in Rome, even if the agreement over the text was only to be reached, as in fact happened, under the Irish presidency.

The 'values of tradition' rest on a history that has lasted more than 50 years. Contrary to what General De Gaulle thought of the 'empty seat' policy, which was deserting the summit during moments of crisis in order to underline the key position of the French, the Italian government, from the post-war period until the present day, has maintained the policy of the 'occupied seat'. This means, first and foremost, to be present, always and everywhere, at the negotiating table and as part of the executive of new institutions. In short, Italy aims to be part of the group of pioneers and founders, in order to appear at the side of other important countries, particularly France and Germany. In the years immediately following the Second World War, Italy's rehabilitation, after 20 years of fascism and the catastrophic alliance with Nazism, could only take place through close cooperation with the United States and with the governments of the Old Continent. For the Italian government, actively participating in the 'European Project' meant leading the country back to being amongst the western democracies, thus recovering legitimacy and a minimum of international visibility. This political line, or doctrine to be more precise, was elaborated and put into effect by Alcide De Gasperi, the Christian Democrat from Trento, who was the first prime minister of the Republican era. This was in tune with two other fundamental figures in the European story, who were also Catholics and frontier men: the French-Alsace Robert Schuman (foreign minister) and the Rhineland German Konrad Adenauer (the German chancellor). Italy was present in Paris on 8 April 1951, when the French, inspired by the Schuman-Monnet duo, hosted the very first ceremony of EU integration: the birth of CECA, the coal and steel pact. Italy was the host on 28 March 1957, when the same six CECA nations – France, Germany, Italy, Holland, Belgium and Luxembourg – gave birth to the EEC, the European Economic Community, in the Hall of the Curiatii and the Horatii on Rome's Capitol Hill.

However, it is true that, through time, the unwavering sense of participation that was there at the beginning (at the time of De Gasperi and Altiero Spinelli, the Prometheus figure of European federalism) has gradually been transformed into habit, routine and inattentive familiarity. Almost all Italian politicians have never ceased to refer to Europe and the institutions in Brussels with complete complaisance. Until a few years ago, this was a ritual of indulgence, as indispensable as it was substantially harmless. After all, what did it take to air some formula drawn out of the store of rhetoric on European integration from time to time and then turn serenely back to the more important domestic issues? At a certain point, the European ideal became a bit like the midday mass for many Catholics: a bland spiritual exercise. Only recently did the European issue become once more a point of discussion, disagreement, and occasional fervour.

In the autumn of 1999, the Commission, led by Romano Prodi, ex-premier of the Italian centre-left coalition, was installed in Brussels. Two years later, in the spring of 2001, his opponent, Berlusconi, arrived at Palazzo Chigi (seat of the executive in Rome) and a new phase in the relationship between Italy and the EU began. Pro-Europeanism and recent Euro-scepticism intersected, alternating on the political stage, even at a few days' interval. Thus, the ceremony of 29 October 2004 added new choreography, ritual and rhetoric to the old European show. Rome and Italy watched the historic signing of the European Constitution for the second time in the Capitol, 47 years after the first, without any particular feeling of excitement. The streets of the centre were closed to traffic. The monuments and ancient ruins seemed to rise in the middle of a disquieting desert, as if they were in a picture by De Chirico. This was not a reflection of indifference but rather that of being accustomed to great European events. They're signing in Italy? What's strange about that? Why shouldn't they?

The speeches made by the heads of state and the government flowed past with images on live television coverage. No one, not even those concerned, were able to recall, even a few hours later, what Jacques Chirac or Tony Blair actually said. Therefore, it was practically taken for granted that the parliamentary debate a few months later would run smoothly and practically without polemics in parliament, in the newspapers and during television debates. Only a few radical groups, dislocated on opposite political formations – the Communist Refoundation Party on the left and Umberto Bossi's Lega Nord on the right – raised any objections. All the other parties gave the green light, contributing to the achievement of an almost plebiscitary result. On 25 January 2005, the Chamber of Deputies approved the ratification of the constitutional treaty with 436 votes in favour, 28 against and 5 abstaining. On 6 April 2005, parliament's other branch, the senate, confirmed approval with 217 voting 'yes' and 16 voting 'no'. Berlusconi had promised that immediately after the October signing Italy would be the first to ratify the treaty. In fact, Italy was seventh, after Lithuania, Hungary, Slovenia, Spain, Latvia and Cyprus. At no point, however, was approval in doubt and the political parties never seriously entertained the idea of a referendum.

The European Constitution has never been a reason for confrontation between the two opposing coalitions, the centre-right led by Berlusconi and Prodi's centre-left. The parliamentary go-ahead marked one of the rare moments that this legislative body has witnessed government and opposition on the same side. Only a few parties openly kept their distance from the mainstream tradition that was summed up, in the course of the Senate debate on 6 April 2005, by the vice president of the House of Deputies, Gianfranco Fini, who had been an active protagonist, on behalf of the Italian government, in the Convention headed by Valery Giscard d'Estaing. In his speech, Fini said, "the favourable vote regarding the Constitution is the logical outcome of the support that the Italian government and parliament have given throughout all the various phases of the long and complex negotiations, consistent with the best Europeanism traditions of our country...It's a matter of our indisputable conviction of the need, above all, to help Europe – finally united on the political field – to take a big step forward on the institutional field, by giving it a solid, shared constitutional base, appropriate to its new geographic and political direction; support for the work of the Convention in which I have had the honour to represent the Italian government and in which the contribution of the Right Honourable Senator (Giuliano) Amato has been both authoritative and decisive, has been constant....The signing of the constitutional treaty – as has been pointed out – did not take place in Rome by chance. It symbolised and continues to be the symbol of an important recognition, of which the Italians are justly proud, of the driving role that our country has had in every phase of the process of European integration." As you can see, Fini took trouble to acknowledge the role of the centre-left, by mentioning the 'contribution' of Senator Giuliano Amato, who was the last prime minister of the Ulivo coalition and vice president in Giscard d'Estaing's European Convention.

On the left, Fausto Bertinotti, secretary of the Communist Refoundation Party and an MEP, tried to dilute the 'bi-partisan' climate by re-proposing a polemic device widespread in other countries, beginning with France. The true Left, claimed Bertinotti, "the part that is most deeply rooted in social concerns and nearest to the no-global movements, can only oppose a 'free trade' constitutional text, in which the market becomes the 'dominus', with respect to politics." Bertinotti's argument, which is the same as that largely employed by the French Socialists, has not made much impact. The confrontation between the 'two Lefts' regarding the prospect of European integration, which is so strongly felt elsewhere in Europe, is not even a leading topic in Italy. During the Senate debate, it was Amato who objected to Bertinotti's analysis, proposing a 'realist' approach to the problem, "although aware that some improvements would have been desirable, an eventual obstruction to the ratification process would mean a backward step for the plan and, in particular, with regard to the safeguarding of social rights, which have been asserted for the first time alongside the market economy".

The approach of the populist right wing, championed by the Lega Nord, has not made inroads either. On the eve of the last local elections, hoping to gain votes, the group led by Umberto Bossi tried to import into Italy the Euro-scepticism doctrine elaborated by Jean-Marie Le Pen in France, rather than that of Jörg Haider in Austria. The electors were painted a gloomy picture of unrestrained immigration, with western identity threatened by the proposed adhesion of Turkey to the EU and family values within the Old Continent put at risk by the diffusion of legalised unions between homosexuals. But once again, this campaign did little to upset the political equilibrium.

Instead, the real novelty is that the movement opposing the tradition is now fishing its arguments out of the economic situation. The controversies regarding 'limits' (intended in the widest sense) feed an anti-European vein that cuts across large segments of the present centre-right majority. This position is represented at the highest level by Giulio Tremonti, former minister of the economy and vice-president in the current Berlusconi government. During television debates, Tremonti often scoffs at the nit-picking nature of European norms: "Brussels even dictates the size of bananas and the volume of boxes of onions." More generally, a portion of the government tends to refer to the EU institutions to explain (and justify) a series of ills that afflict Italian society and the economy, citing arguments like: the Commission is too slow in putting a brake on the import of goods from China, the limits imposed by the Stability Pact hinder business expansion, the hasty introduction of the euro favoured price hikes, and so on.

These types of arguments are beginning to make a breach in public opinion. For many years, Italians have followed European affairs without particular enthusiasm. Even nowadays, few citizens have much idea of the structure of the EU. The European Commission, the Council and even the European Parliament remain, for the majority of people, mysterious concepts. Instead, for some time, the political-economic aspects of Europe have become themes of relative interest. Often the Italians are represented as a people of individualists – indifferent or even uninterested in the res publica. "Governing the Italians isn't difficult. It's simply useless," said Giovanni Giolitti, the historic prime minister, at the beginning of the 20th century. But this judgement, which is possibly rather superficial, does not take into account one simple fact: the Italian electorate is the one that participates more than any other in the whole of Europe at every type of vote. It is, rather, that our situation will lead to the usual paradox.

The European elections of 2004 were dominated, in Italy as elsewhere, by national themes. However, the political elections of 2006, in which the national prime minister will be chosen, will be played out, instead, on European arguments. The 'Italian paradox', that strange mixture of idealised Europeanism and pragmatic Euro-scepticism, contributes to the climate of uncertainty that seems to have substituted the phase of great development, marked by the Convention and the enlargement of the EU to include East European countries.

Germany

Germany, one of the founders of the EU, is traditionally a very pro-European country and everybody expected wide national support for the constitutional treaty. That was the starting point and the treaty was passed with a large majority in the German Bundestag and the Bundesrat. However, the German debate was more about whether the population should be allowed to vote than about the content of the constitutional treaty. Nevertheless, after the French and the Dutch voted 'no', it became clear that there was a growing majority of naysayers among the Germans. The criticism has been concentrated around issues like Europe ought to be closer to and more involved with the people, the focus ought to be on more economic growth and employment, and rethinking rather than rejecting a possible future accession of Turkey.

Still A Loyal Fan, But For How Long?

by Michael Stabenow

Michael Stabenow is a Brussels-based journalist for the Frankfurter Allgemeine Zeitung.

Unlike other heads of European Commission representations in the Member States of the European Union, Gerhard Sabathil enjoyed a relatively relaxed time in the spring of 2005. While his colleagues in Paris and The Hague were anxiously scrutinising alarming opinion polls concerning the forthcoming referendums on the European Constitution, for the head of the Commission's Berlin office it was business as usual. At that stage, from a German perspective at least, nothing seemed to point to the political earthquake which would shake the European Union in the months of May and June.

When, in February 2005, Sabathil responded to the results of a Eurobarometer survey on German public perception of the Constitution, he could state publicly: "A referendum in Germany on the EU Constitution would be mere child's play." Germany, after all, is the archetypal pro-European state, the product of a powerful post-war consensus in favour of close economic and political cooperation to create democracy and prosperity in a peaceful and united Europe.

But how popular is the new European Constitution in Germany in practice? A historically pro-Europe position may not translate simply into a vote for the proposed Constitution. On reflection, could a German referendum really be won so easily? Since this is a hypothetical question, it is difficult to assess whether Sabathil's prediction was realistic or not. Judging from the results of one Eurobarometer survey published in early 2005, which suggested that 79% of Germans were in favour of having a Constitution for Europe, the outcome seemed obvious.[5]

But wanting a constitution of one kind or another is not the same thing as supporting the present draft constitution, which according to Eurobarometer commanded only 54% support with 17% opposed and 28% – almost one in three – undecided. Of course, no one knows if these figures would be reproduced in an actual referendum.

Opinion surveys carried out by the renowned Infratest-Dimap Institute for the German public television network, ARD, revealed that in parallel with the controversial debate ahead of the votes in France and the Netherlands, opinion severely shifted between early May and the middle of June. According to these figures, in early May 59% of Germans backed the Constitution while only 15% opposed it. By late May 52% were in favour of the Constitution while 32% were against it. Finally, figures released by the middle of June, shortly before the opening of the acrimonious Brussels summit meeting, showed for the first time a – slender – majority of 44 to 42% in favour of the opponents.[6]

Why is Germany refusing to consult its citizens directly on this crucial issue? Following the agreement by the heads of state and governments of the European Union on the treaty in June 2004, a controversial and often highly emotional debate on a possible referendum has taken place in Germany. But the proposal was caught up in the turmoil of domestic party political and historical considerations.

The idea of incorporating plebiscitary elements into the German Constitution has long been unpopular and unacceptable to a large proportion of public opinion and policy-makers in Germany. Many contemporary Germans don't like this form of democracy for good historical reasons.

---

[5] Eurobarometer 62, Public Opinion in the European Union, Fieldwork. October/November 2004, Luxembourg 2005-06-20.
[6] Figures drawn from the website http://www.infratest-dimap.de

According to a long-held though increasingly disputed view, the fact that the Constitution of the Weimar Republic contained the possibility of holding referendums is perceived as a factor which helped to pave the way for the Nazi dictatorship in Germany from 1933 to 1945.

That is why the fathers of the basic law, which in 1949 established the second truly German parliamentary democracy after 1919, deliberately enshrined the representative elements of a federal construction with two parliamentary chambers: The Bundestag, the federal parliament and the Bundesrat, the chamber of the now 16 federal states or *Länder*.

Set against this historical background, supporters of the introduction of plebiscitary elements into German political life always had a difficult task. Therefore it was hardly surprising that the incorporation of elements of direct democracy, such as referendums and the citizen's right of initiative or petition (supported by the federal government of Social Democrats and Greens after coming to power in 1998 and again after re-election in 2002), have not materialised. The idea of a referendum was staunchly defended by some German constitutionalists such as Hans-Herbert von Arnim and Jörn Ipsen, and non-party grass-roots organisations such as Mehr Demokratie (More Democracy) which has around 3,700 members.

Results of an opinion poll by the Infratest-Dimap Institute published in 2004 showed that more than two-thirds of German voters favoured a referendum on the Constitution. At party political level, the only force supporting a referendum openly and early was the liberal FDP. But their proposal to hold a referendum was voted down in November 2003 by 528 out of 584 members of the Bundestag.

With an increasing number of other Member States going for a referendum, the discussion became very agitated again in the summer and autumn of 2004. The fact that a central precondition for constitutional changes is a two-thirds majority in both chambers (Bundestag and Bundesrat) meant that such a decision needed large cross-party support and would be subject to tactical political party considerations. At the end of October 2004, the SPD and Greens presented a common proposal to introduce, in general terms, the possibility of holding national referendums into the German Constitution – thus going far beyond the idea of a popular vote just on the European constitutional treaty.

The largest opposition party, the Christian Democrats (CDU) saw this as a purely tactical move in order to create a split with its Bavarian sister party, the CSU and the FDP (its potential ally in government). Like the Liberals, the prime minister of Bavaria, Edmund Stoiber (CSU), had also come out in favour of a referendum on the Constitution – the difference being that he was linking it to the (unrealistic) condition of a Europe-wide referendum. This again came close to the position of the Greens.

Critics who had argued that a move in August 2004 by the federal chancellor, Gerhard Schröder (SPD), and the SPD party chairman, Franz Müntefering, in favour of a vote on the European Constitution was of a purely tactical nature were finally proved right in December 2004. The coalition partners decided not to introduce the bill for the time being in the Bundestag. This meant, as Müntefering publicly confirmed in January 2005, that there would be no referendum on the EU Constitution in Germany.

In an e-mail, written in July 2004 to the members of the SPD parliamentary group in the Bundestag, the powerful chairman had clearly stated his rejection of a referendum on the constitutional treaty. "We will take the decision on the EU Constitution within the institutions which, according to our well-tested basic law, are responsible for it: these are the Bundestag and Bundesrat. Our Constitution doesn't foresee any other possibility."[7]

Müntefering's letter is probably an accurate reflection of the general unease felt in Germany among a majority of the political elite. As in other countries, there was widespread fear that a referendum would not really focus on a complex 480-page treaty, but on other issues not directly related to it, such as the question of accession of Turkey to the EU. The main argument was that a referendum on the Constitution would be mistaken for a domestic popularity test for the government. Although the picture was more mixed in the German media, the sceptical official view was largely shared.

In the German weekly *Die Zeit*, Bernd Ulrich argued in favour of the traditional 'representative' approach and warned against the possible consequences of a referendum: "Politics would become more populist, and beside the Bundestag and the Bundesrat, a third chamber would emerge: the plebiscite was the *Bild-Zeitung*'s revenge against what remains of rational discourse within the political system."[8]

Pro-European credentials in Germany, one of the six founding members of the Community, have become less clear-cut than in the preceding decades. While accession of the Central and Eastern European former communist countries was seen as a logical step for a country which, in 1990, a year after the fall of the Berlin wall, had overcome a 45-year long split, concerns grew about the practical implications of enlargement. This mainly applied to the possible influx of people from neighbouring countries onto a labour market at a historical post-war high of more than 5 million unemployed in early

---

[7] Quoted from *Frankfurter Allgemeine Zeitung*, 28 July 2004.
[8] *Die Zeit,* 29 July 2004.

2005. Although the government supports the accession of Turkey, the idea of its membership remains very controversial in Germany.

Finally, domestic policy developments have led to increasing tension between the federal government and the European Commission. Chancellor Gerhard Schröder, under pressure at home in the opinion polls, had launched a number of attacks, chiefly on the European Commission. This concerned, for example, the planned EU regulation of the chemical industry, REACH (Registration, Evaluation and Authorisation of Chemicals) or, as in France, the controversial proposal for a directive on services. An increasing number of disputes have helped to consolidate a picture of an anonymous European bureaucracy (often simply called 'Brussels' in an undifferentiated and disparaging way).

The main argument with the Berlin government over the past years was over the application of the budget deficit criteria for the European Monetary Union, which finally resulted in an overhaul of the European stability and growth pact in March 2005. With the support of a good deal of the domestic media, the German government also managed to get the message across that the core of the problem was in the restrictive rules of the pact rather than in a lack of budgetary restraint. In spite of a show of pro-European rhetoric, the view was also widely shared that the European Commission should not ask for extra money for the Community budget in the coming years when, at the same time, it was seeking to impose spending curbs at a domestic level.

However, on balance, today's generation of politicians largely remain aware of and convinced about the crucial historical, economic, and political role of the integration process for Germany and for Europe. Historically, the rapid inclusion of Western Germany after 1945 into the European project served as a catalyst for reintegrating the country in the family of civilised nations and thus spurring the economic and political stabilisation of post-war Germany.

Establishing the country in the western hemisphere was a project that divided the political class. While the Christian Democrats (the CDU and its Bavarian sister party, the CSU) and Liberals (FDP) clearly had supported the move since the late Forties, the opposition Social Democrats (SPD) showed little enthusiasm at first.

The SPD was caught between its internationalist tradition and its refusal to envisage a perspective towards German reunification through linking the western part unilaterally to the European Institutions and NATO. By the time the SPD had adopted its reformist 'Godesberger Programme' in November 1959, the party had already begun to move towards a pro-integration course that it has pursued ever since. But it was only after the

SPD had formed a coalition government with the CDU and CSU in 1966 and its chairman, Willy Brandt, had become foreign minister that the party turned into a driving force for the integration process.

The main foundation of German European politics, sometimes misunderstood by its partners, remains reconciliation and partnership with France. In spite of frequently conflicting traditions and visions stemming from French centralism and German federalism, leaders of successive generations in both countries have always tried to forge common positions on most of the crucial European issues. This was already true in the Fifties when there was a trade-off between building a common (later single) market on the one hand, in the interests of Germany's export orientated industry, and a Common Agricultural policy (CAP) on the other, catering to French interests.

That is why, while advocating budgetary restraint, even in the autumn of 2002, Germany backed a political compromise on the reform of the CAP designed in the first place to preserve French farming interests and fixing farm spending through the EU budget until 2013. This agreement, reached during the Danish EU Presidency, was a French precondition for opening the door for the accession Central and Eastern European countries.

Without the famous Franco-German axis, symbolised by such contrasting 'couples' as Valéry Giscard d´Estaing and Helmut Schmidt in the Seventies, François Mitterrand and Helmut Kohl in the Eighties and Nineties and later Jacques Chirac and Gerhard Schröder, the European integration process of the past decades would have been inconceivable. This also goes for moves towards monetary and political union, German reunification (after some initial French hesitation) and finally the agreement on the European Constitution.

The evolution from a Community of six founding members to a European Union comprising 25 members "reflecting the will of the citizens and States of Europe" (Article I-1 of the constitutional treaty), has also had an effect on the way that European integration is perceived in Germany. To a larger extent than in other countries, a parallel was drawn between developments at the national and European levels. It seemed only logical that the German experience of establishing a bicameral federal system with a strong parliament – first gaining budgetary, then legislative rights and finally, full constitutional authority – should serve as a blueprint for European integration.

Many of the contributions of leading German politicians in the past were highly influenced by this traditional federalist approach. This is true for the 1996 proposal by Karl Lamers and Wolfgang Schäuble, leading CDU politicians on European affairs, calling for a "core Europe", and for Foreign Minister Joschka Fischer's speech at Berlin's Humboldt University on the "Federation of Nation States" in May 2000. Likewise, in April 2001, in a European strategy paper for the SPD, even Chancellor Schröder pledged for a "strong European executive", turning the European Commission into a fully-fledged government in a federal Europe.[9]

On the other hand, the famous judgement of the German Constitutional Court of October 1993 on the Maastricht Treaty had specified limits to integration, by refuting the concept of a federal 'European state' based on a 'European people', rather than talking of an association of states ('Staatenverbund'). In April 2005, Peter Gauweiler, a member of the Bundestag for the Bavarian CSU and a staunch supporter of a referendum on the Constitution in Germany, decided to seize the Constitutional Court judgement, mainly arguing that the constitutional treaty amounted to a deprivation of rights of the Bundestag. On 15 June, the federal president, Horst Köhler, announced that he would not process the corresponding ratification law before a decision of the Constitutional Court.

Another case relating to the role of the European arrest warrant and the possibility of enforcing laws of one Member State in another first came before the court in mid April. The forthcoming judgement could have a major impact on the way Germany deals with further integration.

While this case, which has attracted a great deal of attention in the media, is in the hands of the federal judges, politicians seem more concerned with the respective powers of the parliamentary institutions to apply the provisions of the European Constitution within Germany. Except for the former communists (PDS) and a minority of the Bavarian CSU, no party is opposing the Constitution. In spring 2005, some German academics, such as the economist Roland Vaubel from Mannheim and the Berlin law professor Christian Kirchner, had signed a public declaration of the 'European Constitutional Group' arguing that the Constitution should be rejected on the grounds that it is, for example, furthering centralisation and increasing the distance between the citizens and those who exercise power in the name of the people.

More generally speaking from a German point of view, one of the major achievements of the constitutional treaty is the establishment of rules clarifying the subsidiarity principle and giving national parliaments – to

---

[9] Quoted from a speech by Gerhard Schröder "Verantwortung für Europa", SPD-Leitantrag of 30 April 2001.

both chambers in Germany – a say in European legislation, and even the right to challenge it before the European Court of Justice.

Criticism raised by CDU and CSU politicians mainly centred on the role of the *Länder* in European decision-making, but not on the Constitution as such. However, probably also responding to the controversial debate on the Constitution in neighbouring countries like France and the Netherlands, there were also more fundamental criticisms raised by a number of politicians, chiefly from the ranks of CDU and CSU. Some argued against a 'democratic deficit' in the Constitution; others insisted on the lack of a clear reference to God in the constitutional treaty.

In spite a number of critical remarks expressed in written explanations to the vote in the Bundestag, an overwhelming majority of 569 out of 594 members (more than 95%) taking part in the vote approved the constitutional treaty on 12 May. Twenty-three members voted against and two abstained. On 27 May, two days before the French referendum, the Bundesrat also approved the Constitution.

And what about the German citizens? Since there will be no referendum on the Constitution their views will continue to be expressed through opinion polls like Eurobarometer. According to the figures cited at the outset by the Commission's Head of Office in Berlin at the beginning of 2005, the picture seemed clear with 79% of German citizens aged over 15 in favour of having a European Constitution. Only Belgians and Slovenians were indisputably more favourable than the Germans (with 81% and 80% respectively). Asked directly about the constitutional treaty signed in October 2004 in Rome, 54% of Germans replied that they favoured it and 17% opposed it while 28% were undecided, of whom some would probably vote in favour if put to the test. This placed Germany ninth out of 25 Member States in terms of its support for the Constitution.

The same opinion poll revealed a worrying feature for the future. Less than a year after accession of ten new Member States, 60% of Germans replied to a question that the current number of European Member States was 12 (and not 25). A simple mistake of this sort would hardly have been made by the majority of Germans who gave such strong support to the signing of the original Treaty of Rome.

This sort of misconception might also contribute to explaining why the general state of awareness of Europe and its impact on the daily lives of German citizens is now more fluid and opinion increasingly volatile and often ill-informed. However, it cannot be denied that the French and Dutch no-votes on the constitutional treaty have changed the nature of the debate on Europe in Germany. This was reinforced by the general expectation of a change of government in Berlin after the general elections foreseen for September 2005.

Criticism by the CDU and CSU politicians centred on the question of moving Europe closer to the citizen, concentrating on ways to help growth and employment, and to rethink, delay – or rather scrap – the process of integrating Turkey into the European Union. Unease about the way Europe had developed could be clearly sensed among 'the man in the street' as television programmes illustrated. However, in the wake of the fundamental debate on the pros and cons of European integration, Germany's political class seemed to have become aware of the threats to basic achievements of European integration since 1945.

It can be argued that this has led Chancellor Schröder to show his readiness for a compromise on the EU budget for the period from 2007 to 2013, even before the Brussels summit in June had got underway. This was the same politician who, in autumn 1998 when the SPD and Green Party joined forces to form a coalition, appeared at best lukewarm in his support for European integration. And it was the same politician who had helped, earlier in 2005, to undermine the European stability and growth pact and who, by continuously attacking plans and decisions by the European Commission, contributed to reinforce public unease about 'Brussels' in Germany.

By June 2005, Schröder found himself back in the role of powerful defender of the Community, its institutions, and warning against what was perceived as a strategy pursued chiefly by British Prime Minister Tony Blair to limit Europe's scope to that of a free trade zone. "This Europe can only survive as a political union," Schröder said at his final press conference at the Brussels summit.

The CDU chairwoman, Angela Merkel, who by the summer of 2005 looked set to become Germany's next chancellor, also sought to reassure partners on the country's future stance on Europe. Speaking on 20 June in Berlin, she warned against pinning the goals of achieving economic growth and political union against each other. But in order to accept Europe as a political union, citizens needed reassurances that the EU cared about their economic wealth. In essence, Merkel described Germany's task as that of an "honest broker".

For both Schröder and Merkel in the early days of summer 2005, the challenge for Germany seemed clear: France and the Netherlands seemed paralysed through their referendums and Prime Minister Blair had appeared to find himself at the beginning of the British EU presidency in a not too 'splendid isolation'. There was a sense that Germany, in its capacity as a large and founding member of the Community, seemed prepared to assume its responsibility in helping to reshape the European Union, while at the same time preserving the historical and political vision of the integration process.

Denmark

Had the Danish referendum about the constitutional treaty been held according to plan on 27 September 2005, the signs, at least in the earlier stages of the debate, were that the Danes would have voted 'yes'. Nevertheless, there is a persistent EU opposition, which has been expressed in the six referendums held in Denmark on EU questions. The Danes, who fear surrender of sovereignty, paradoxically enough keep electing politicians who are overwhelmingly pro-European. In practice, this has evolved into a bipartisan political system. One system is based on referendums, where the people directly decide the big European questions. The other system is parliamentary: politicians in the Danish parliament decide on everything else, including those EU questions that will not be voted on in a national referendum.

Referendum – The Wrong Answer To An Important Question

by Tøger Seidenfaden

Tøger Seidenfaden is editor-in-chief of Politiken.

It could have been a 'yes' in the Danish referendum on the European Constitution, had it been going to take place on 27 September 2005. Certainly polls had suggested a better chance of a positive outcome than in France or Holland, where the 'no' prevailed, or in the UK where a 'no' would have been the probable response. The Danish expectation is based on the fact that the left-wing party, which has historically been at the core of Danish opposition to the EU, has now joined a broad parliamentarian consensus, and will campaign for the 'yes'. However, getting that party, the Socialistic People's Party (SF), to vote 'yes', though significant, is in some ways solving a problem of the past. Anti-European feelings in Denmark used to be mainly found among left-wing voters. In recent years, however, it is right-wing opposition that has been growing. Also, the Danish left as a whole is historically weak, having polled only 35% of the votes in the February 2005 election. Even without the French-Dutch debacle, which led to immediate no-majorities in several Danish polls, opposition to the

Constitution, which had been as low as 30%, could have been expected to rise.

Holding referendums about the EU is perhaps the only area in which Denmark is unambiguously ahead of most of its European partners in terms of political and practical experience. Between October 1972 and September 2000, Denmark has held six referendums on Europe. Only Ireland has held just as many. The fact is even more remarkable when one considers that Denmark is not a referendum-holding country. Indeed, apart from finally lowering the voting age to 18 in 1978, no other referendums have been held in the whole period. In the six referendums held, the 'ayes' have had it four times (1972, 1986, 1993 and 1998) and the 'nays' twice (1992 and 2000).

From the perspective of national politics, including all the representative institutions of society (trade unions, employer and business organisations, NGOs, media, etc.) the Danish story is one of an initially broad, pro-European consensus that grows broader and broader. Only in 1986 did two major, so-called responsible parties (i.e. parties that have participated in governments, and could do so in the future), pick the no-side and, paradoxically, in that referendum the yes-side won handsomely, despite a majority of sceptics in parliament. Apart from that episode, all the main parties have consistently been pro-EU and the level of support for European treaties in parliament has never fallen much below the 80% level. It has never been possible, and it is not possible now, to form a government in Denmark that would not be solidly pro-EU.

However, if one looks at the six referendums, they are a history of sustained opposition in the electorate, an opposition that has risen twice to the level of rejection. This gap between the elected politicians and their voters is the central feature of Danish European politics, and both sides of the gap should be constantly kept in mind. The organised political and social forces in Denmark are overwhelmingly and increasingly pro-European. The electorate, on the other hand, is unpredictable in the context of a long series of referendums. The fact that the politicians have not managed to convince the voters is significant – but equally noticeable and significant is the fact that the voters have not managed to convince the politicians. In fact, when voting for parliament, they have consistently re-elected a set of politicians, only to largely reject their advice when a referendum comes up.

The Danish debate on Europe began, in parallel with the British debate, in a context dominated by market access. The UK was historically Denmark's most important trade partner, but the continental economies were becoming more important. If the UK joined the Common Market, there was no real question that Denmark had to follow. It was a matter of economics:

agricultural price supports were attractive and market access for industrial goods was decisive for the future of a modernising economy. Politically, the background was more complex. Denmark had a long tradition of neutrality coming out of the 19th century. After the experience of occupation by Nazi Germany in 1940-45, neutrality was replaced by membership of NATO in 1949. Having chosen its side in the cold war, many Danish politicians were anxious to limit the consequences of that choice: no foreign bases were established, and Denmark was supposedly nuclear free (though Greenland was secretly put at the disposal of the US). This mind-set made many people, especially on the political left, see the Common Market as a form of power politics, which would threaten Denmark's quiet life as a low key, appeasing, albeit Atlanticist, actor in the cold war. In 1972, opposition to the EEC was effectively confined to communists, the new left, and dissidents within the main Social Democratic and Centrist (Social Liberal) Parties.

The Danish Constitution stipulates that a treaty involving a transfer of sovereignty from Denmark to international institutions can be approved in two ways: either by a vote in parliament with a five-sixths majority, or through a referendum with a simple majority of those polled. In 1971, when the issue of Danish accession arose, there was, in fact, a five-sixths majority in parliament. But, to avoid a divisive internal debate with his left wing, the leader of the Social Democratic Party (who became prime minister later that year) asked for a referendum. The tripartite government made up of Social Liberals, Agrarian Liberals, and Conservatives reluctantly accepted this. After an emotional campaign, where the left managed to get a majority for the 'no' in the capital, Copenhagen, the 'yes' won by a decisive margin (56.7% voted 'yes' and 32.9% voted 'no'). There was a very high participation rate of close to 90% of voters. In terms of referendum support for the yes-campaign, it has been downhill from there.

Until the 1990s, the pattern remained the same: broad establishment support, but opposition on the left, both inside and outside of parliament. In 1986, the Social Democrats and Social Liberals rather opportunistically defected from supporting the European Single Act. However, the government turned the tables on them by calling a highly unusual consultative referendum on the treaty in which a majority, in effect, confirmed Danish support for the EU. This re-established the pro-European consensus, which was further strengthened with the end of the cold war, and thus removed the ambiguities which had limited support for the European community on the left and in the formerly neutralist centre. By 1992, the Danish centre-left had become as solidly pro-European as the centre-right, and the mood among intellectuals, academics and opinion-makers was moving in the same direction.

The electorate, however, was another matter. Several new factors came into play. For the first time, the EU was presented as a mainly political enterprise, a process involving the (re-)unification of Europe based on values. Impressed by the new Europe emerging in 1989-91, politicians and academics were pleased about this. The electorate, however, had been told for twenty years that the EU was an economic arrangement, that we were in it for the money, and that issues like sovereignty and supra-nationalism had no real relevance. Now, it turned out, they had. At the same time, the far right in Danish politics was a new factor. Since 1973 it had been represented by a populist, libertarian, anti-tax and pro-European party. By 1992, this had been replaced by the Danish Peoples Party (DF), which remains populist but is xenophobic rather than libertarian and is, as a nationalistic party, strongly anti-European. At the same time, the mostly leftwing 'no' movements acquired new, less partisan themes, accepted membership of the EU as such, but continued to refuse new treaties on the grounds of fear of centralisation, loss of sovereignty and lack of democracy. The result was a popular no-vote, by the narrowest of margins, in the Maastricht referendum of June 1992. In this crisis, the only way to broaden the yes-coalition was to convert the left, specifically the SF, which, in accordance with the zeitgeist, already contained a number of closet pro-Europeans. In 1993, the SF duly advocated a yes-vote; however, in 1998 it reverted to a no-position, a position which it stuck to until the vote in 2000 on the referendum. Finally, it reached its pro-European destination in December 2004. Since this was endorsed by more than 60% of its members in an internal, postal referendum, it is likely to move more voters than earlier, more divided and tactical pronouncements by a divided leadership have done. However, the party leader who pulled it off has now resigned as a consequence of not reversing a long-term, if moderate, decline in voter support in the parliamentary elections of February 2005. It may take some time before the SF becomes a truly effective participant in the broad yes-coalition. Nevertheless, the consolidation of left-wing support will help stabilise the Social Democratic vote, where many voters have traditionally felt unable to follow their now unanimously pro-European leadership.

But would this have been enough to ensure a 'yes' to the Constitution?

If a referendum ever takes place in Denmark, the yes-side will wage a campaign based mainly on the content of the constitutional treaty. It will underline that it contains a consolidation and modernisation of previous treaties, and a more efficient and transparent decision-making system. Having a permanent chairman (not president), a real foreign minister and the simpler double-majority voting system, which does not weaken Danish influence, will also be underlined. The fact that the treaty now makes it clear that the union is the instrument of nation-states (not the other way round), and that there is now a procedure for leaving the union, will also be seen as advantages. More broadly, the constitutional treaty will be sold as necessary for decision-making in an enlarged EU, even though, of course, both the Amsterdam and Nice Treaties were also sold in this way.

The far right in the form of the Danish People's Party stands ready to wage a strong no-campaign on two main fronts: refusal of the idea of Turkish membership of the EU and concern about the arrival of new, lower-paid workers from new EU member countries like Poland, the Baltic republics and so on. Ironically, these issues have nothing to do with the treaty, being a consequence of agreements of the past, or of agreements yet to come. As has been seen in other member countries, this in itself does not render them ineffective in the public debate that is taking place. Of course, any remaining uncertainty about a final French, Dutch or other national ratification would also be exploited to the hilt by opponents to the treaty. Just like in the UK, fear of isolation within the EU has always been part of the yes-arsenal. After the French and Dutch, it is doubtful if such an argument can ever be fully effective again.

It is also worth asking to what extent the left-right prism is really the only relevant one, or even the most important one, when it comes to analysing and predicting the dynamics of a referendum campaign. Though the balance of opposition in Denmark is clearly shifting from left to right, the most effective arguments on the no-side have always been those that in some sense transcend the left-right divide, or which are at least compatible with both right and left-wing rhetoric – especially of the populist kind. Two or three themes predominate. The most basic one is of course sovereignty, where the fear of losing national control can be mobilised within most, if not all, political ideologies. The second one is openness, where right-wingers fear foreigners of all kinds, while parts of the left are concerned with wage-levels and social dumping. A possible third is centralisation and bureaucracy, which can again be given prominence from both ends of the political spectrum. These 'evergreens' of EU opposition can be mobilised in the context of any treaty, since some degree of sovereignty-pooling, open borders and administrative centralisation will always be part of the EU enterprise.

What is even more striking in the Danish experience of repeated referendums is the rise of issues that not only have nothing to do with the treaty at hand, but nor with EU-policy as such. It is noticeable that what one might call procedural issues, which all in some sense revolve around the issue of trust, have become more and more dominant as one referendum has succeeded another. At the same time, voter patterns have come to reflect sociological differences in the population, rather than party political differences. The yes-voter is well-educated, relatively affluent, lives in major cities and, most importantly, has confidence in the future. The no-voter on the other hand is disaffected with less education, less money and worried about the future. In Denmark, women are also more likely to vote 'no' than men are.

The overriding issue is trust – or rather distrust – in the political class as a whole. Paradoxically, the use of what many consider the most direct and legitimate form of popular participation – the referendum – in practice produces mistrust between the electorate and their politicians. Of course, mistrust of politicians is not unusual in EU and other democracies. But in Denmark, general political mistrust is in fact comparatively low – except on the EU issue. But in this area, mistrust is being created because of the disjunction of the political system. In effect, two systems have been created: one, referendum-based, for dealing with the basic European issues; the other, parliamentarian, for dealing with everything else, including EU policy between referendums. One obvious consequence is that no-votes are bound to be 'betrayed' by the majority, the yes-politicians. Not because of moral turpitude, but because they have been elected in the parliamentarian political system on a pro-EU platform, and most therefore minimise the consequences, and indeed prepare the grounds for reversing a no-result as soon as it occurs. At the same time, most of the actors on the no-side are either not in the parliamentarian political system, or are marginal in it. They can thus wage 'irresponsible' campaigns; in the strict sense that they will not be in charge of the consequences, and do not have to develop a national policy to deal with them. Interestingly, the 'original sin' in Danish EU-policy can be traced to the same disjuncture. Why did Danish proponents of joining Europe, as mentioned above, only emphasise the economic rationale? After all, some of them also supported the vision of political unity and internationalisation underlying the whole enterprise. The answer is that they were being loyal to the broad parliamentarian compromise supporting the Danish application. And that compromise, to be as broad as possible, naturally expressed the lowest common denominator for support, i.e. the economic advantages. If the public was misled, it was not because of the intrinsic mendaciousness of politicians, but because it reflected the very different logic of the parliamentarian system, a logic that in the longer run has shown itself to be both ineffective and vulnerable in the free-for-all of charge and counter-charge that constitutes the substance of a referendum campaign.

It has been an eerie experience for Danish observers of the French and Dutch referendum campaigns, to see how many of these patterns – with variations due to local circumstances – have played themselves out in two very different European polities. Sceptical Dutch and French voters have sounded exactly like the Danish voters of 1992 (and 2000), right down to the rhetoric ("Is it forbidden to vote 'no', then?" being an example seen in all three countries, when confronted with increasingly desperate, heavyweight arguments from the yes-side). Mistrust has been at the core of French and Dutch dynamics, and so have many of the above-mentioned handicaps of the yes-side. Pending further study, I would already assert that the inbuilt advantage of the no-side in any EU referendum campaign has been strongly confirmed by these two dramatic upsets for united political establishments.

Holding a referendum does not guarantee a no-vote. But nor does overwhelming political support in the ordinary political system guarantee success in this very different arena. This is the Danish experience, and the ten EU countries that have arranged a referendum on the Constitution, knowing full well that a single 'no' is enough to unleash a full-scale political crisis, might have done well to ponder the implications before they did so. The present nightmarish steeplechase from unpredictable referendum to unpredictable referendum has ended in a double 'no' and a suspended process. Had the Danish and Irish experience been considered earlier, this might have been avoided. One must hope it is not too late to learn from our collective European mistakes.

Arranging referendums may be thought of, beyond accidental and constitutional political circumstances, as an attempt to respond to the very real challenge of political legitimacy in an increasingly powerful EU. The Danish experience, coming as it does from an otherwise highly mature, functional and democratically successful society, strongly suggests that the referendum is the wrong answer to a very real question. The disasters for the EU adventure that have struck in France and the Netherlands may finally be bringing this home to EU leaders as a whole. If the referendum route kills the Constitution and even if, miraculously and fortuitously, it does not, Europe will have to devise a better and more responsible answer to a very serious question. If the EU is to have a future, that is.

The United Kingdom

In the United Kingdom, the question about Europe has always been viewed as a political football that could be kicked around in an unpredictable game of domestic politics. Tony Blair, paradoxically enough, promised the British people a referendum about the constitutional treaty in order to plug the holes in the EU debate, which could have damaged him politically before the British national election. The EU question is a dangerous topic in the domestic political debate because the British are among some of the EU's strongest critics. They fear surrendering their sovereignty, the EU's bureaucracy and refuge policies as well as economic cost disadvantages. Although they are unafraid of an in-breadth enlargement, they do not want an in-depth enlargement. Thus, for Blair, it was anything but a tragedy that France and the Netherlands voted 'no' and thereby put the constitutional treaty into cold storage.

The EU As A Political Football In A Game Of Domestic Politics

by Jonathan Steele

Jonathan Steele is the Guardian's Senior Foreign Correspondent and an international affairs columnist.

The United Kingdom is a stranger to referendums. They are not part of the British tradition and only one has been held in the last 50 years. The referendum on the UK's membership in the European Economic Community in 1975 was not only unique in British terms, but it was unlike any other held in continental Europe, since voters were not asked in advance of entry, in other words whether they wanted their country to join the EEC. The United Kingdom had already entered the EEC in 1973 after a parliamentary vote the previous year. The question put to British voters in 1975 was whether they wanted to stay in. This odd sequence of events highlights the fact that Europe has always been a political football in the UK. When governments and opposition parties promise referendums on Europe, they do it as a way of embarrassing their rivals or scoring points for themselves. It was true in the 1970s and it remains true today in the crisis over the EU Constitution.

The UK's only referendum came about because Harold Wilson unexpectedly defeated Edward Heath, the most Europhile prime minister Britain has ever had, in 1974. Wilson led a Labour party, which was deeply divided over Europe, and he favoured the UK's EEC membership but during the election campaign he said he would "renegotiate" the UK's membership and put the results to a referendum. This seemed to him the only way to deal with the party's internal divisions. European leaders accepted a number of minor changes as part of the British renegotiation and the national vote was held. Although the government recommended a yes-vote, cabinet ministers were allowed a free choice. There was no party whip. During the referendum campaign, some ministers campaigned for a yes-vote, others pressed for a 'no'.

The same double act was played on the Conservative party side, with leading figures in the no- and the yes-camps. The major broadsheet newspapers supported the UK's membership, as did the main employers' organisation while the Trade Union Congress was against. The no-side counterpoised the EEC to the Commonwealth, which was a more powerful body in those days. Would Britain be turning its back on traditional allies like Australia and New Zealand, and have to raise tariffs on their exports, so that the country would end up eating Danish rather than New Zealand butter, they asked? In the end the vote was a heavy endorsement of Europe, with 67% voting for the UK to stay in.

When Margaret Thatcher took power in 1979, Europe continued to be a divisive issue. She had voted 'yes' to Europe in the referendum but as prime minister, she became increasingly Euro-sceptic. Although she went along with moves towards greater European integration, she did it with reluctance, always arguing for the narrow British interest at every European Council she attended. Her Conservative successor, John Major, reaped the bitter harvest she had planted. Even though he insisted on a British opt-out in the 1992 Maastricht Treaty, which paved the way for monetary union, he had great difficulty in getting parliament to ratify the treaty. There were scenes verging on farce as Major struggled with a small majority of 18 seats in the Commons while the Conservative 'Maastricht' rebels numbered 22. MPs were dragged out of hospital to vote and on one occasion, Chris Patten, suffering from gastroenteritis, was brought into the Commons in a wheel chair. Trying to bring Major down, the Labour party voted against ratification, even though most of its leaders supported the principles of the Maastricht Treaty. In the end, Major got it through in July 1993 with the Commons split down the middle, 317 to 317. The speaker of the House of Commons, who is traditionally a member of the largest party in parliament but who rarely votes since his primary job is to be an impartial chair of parliament's sessions, was forced off the fence. He supported the government so the treaty squeaked through and Major remained in office.

With Europe clearly a highly contentious issue it was no surprise that the referendum weapon came back into play. It was first taken up again by a maverick right-winger, Sir James Goldsmith, who had dual British and French citizenship and was a member of the European Parliament for the 'Europe of Nations' party. A confirmed Euro-sceptic, he announced in November 1994 that he was going to found a political party to campaign for a British referendum on the UK's EU membership. Two years later, the new leader of the Labour party, Tony Blair, also came out with a promise of a referendum. Blair was, in broad terms, a Europhile who favoured the principle of British membership, quite unlike Goldsmith. But he saw the advantages of a referendum. It could get you off the hook of tough decisions. It could embarrass your opponents, and it could gain time. So in 1996 in the run-up to the general election, which would have to be held in the spring of 1997 at the latest, he gave his promise. The nation would be able to have its say. There was no chance that a majority of British voters would support UK entry into the euro-zone, and the referendum promise was purely a tactical way of neutralising the issue in the election campaign, and removing fears that a Labour victory would mean automatic UK entry.

Labour won the election, and in the autumn of 1997 Blair and his chancellor of the exchequer, Gordon Brown, said that, in addition to a referendum, the British government would have to be satisfied with five economic conditions before it would recommend adoption of the euro. Meanwhile, Goldsmith's Referendum party won 800,000 votes in the 1997 election. It was not enough to win a seat in parliament but it was an impressive number of votes for a new party.

In spite of broad support for Europe, highlighted in Blair's phrase that Britain must "be at the heart of Europe", the Labour government shared Major's view that it was better to "widen" rather than "deepen" Europe. Sceptical over moves towards greater integration for fear it would eventually lead to a federal Europe, Blair supported EU membership for the former Communist countries of Eastern Europe, as well as the Balkans and Turkey. Britain's cautious stance on integration came out clearly in the debates at the European convention and in the intergovernmental discussions that preceded the adoption of the European Constitution. Britain laid down a number of 'red lines' that it would not cross. In the White Paper, which the government published once the text of the Constitution was agreed, Jack Straw, the Foreign Secretary, boasted that nearly half the changes negotiated in the last stages of drafting the Constitution were British initiatives. He described this as "a measure of the influence Britain had on its final form". On another occasion, he called the Constitution "a British vision for Europe". Given that any government is bound to put the best possible gloss on an international treaty, these were still extraordinary claims.

Straw was proud that Britain had resisted the extension of qualified majority voting to some new areas such as defence, social security, and the EU budget, thereby "preserving the British veto". It had insisted that, for NATO's members, NATO remained the foundation of any common European security and defence policy. In general, the Blair government argued that the Constitution improved the functioning of Europe's institutions by giving more power to the European Parliament, and creating a European president. As the constitution-drafting process was reaching its climax, several EU Member States promised their electorates referendums. In April 2004, Blair announced that there would be one in Britain also. His move puzzled some commentators. When he had promised a referendum on the euro back in 1996, Labour was still in opposition. Offering voters a choice looked like a defensive move, designed to forestall pre-emptive attacks. In 2004, by contrast, Labour was in power and apparently sailing towards a third election victory. The Conservatives were trailing a long way behind in the polls. At the previous election in 2001, when their leader William Hague campaigned on the issue of "saving the pound", the electorate had been unmoved. Hague was easily beaten.

Nevertheless, Europe has never been an entirely predictable issue in Britain. The country's underlying Euro-scepticism can break out at any moment. In 2004, the Conservatives' new leader, Michael Howard, was promising a referendum on the Constitution. A new party, the United Kingdom Independence Party (which was formed after Goldsmith's death) was doing well in the polls and it went on to win several seats in the European Parliament elections that summer. Blair had initially dismissed the Constitution as "a tidying-up exercise" without major importance. So his decision to offer this allegedly minor document to a referendum – as we have seen, a rare event in British parliamentary history – looked odd. As time went on, his decision seemed more and more like a gamble. Persuading the British public to vote for the Constitution was going to be an uphill struggle. A Eurobarometer poll done in November 2004 found Britain was more hostile to the Constitution than any of the other 24 Member States. Thirty per cent said they opposed it compared to 20% in favour. In France, ironically given the actual vote that took place six months later on 29 May, only 17% were opposed and 48% were in favour. The findings for the Netherlands were 11% against and 63% in favour.

Who exactly are the Constitution's opponents in Britain? An ICM poll in March 2004 showed the type of person most likely to vote 'no' was a lower middle-class woman in her late 50s or early 60s living in the English Midlands. While two-thirds of those polled were against the Constitution, the better educated and better off were more likely to vote for it. Among the so-called AB class, mainly consisting of professional people and managers, 28% were in favour and 51% against, while among unskilled manual workers and the unemployed support for the Constitution came from only 25% with 58% against.

However, the good news for pro-Europeans was that if the question was whether Britons wanted to leave the EU altogether, there was a strong majority for staying in among people at the top and bottom of the social pyramid. Only among skilled manual workers, so-called C2s, did the anti-EU people narrowly exceed the pro-EU ones.

In Britain, the argument over the EU is largely couched in terms of sovereignty: whether "unelected Brussels bureaucrats" take too many decisions without reference to the British parliament, and impose directives on countries without consultation. Opponents of the Constitution fear the EU will take charge of asylum and other contentious issues, thereby forcing Britain to do things it would not otherwise wish to do. In general, there is a sense that the EU costs Britain too much money. So it was hardly surprising that Blair abstained from naming a date for the referendum he had promised. He tried to postpone it as long as possible, saying only that it would be sometime in 2006, very close to the October 2006 deadline.

By February 2005 when ICM did its next poll, the figures had barely changed. The no-vote for the Constitution had 54% support, while the 'yes' only had 26%. Again, most support came from the AB class, professionals and managers, while C2 voters were hostile. Young people were not as hostile as the old. Among the 18 to 24-year olds, 24% said 'yes', and 16% 'no', with a huge percentage still undecided. The next age range, from 25 to 34, was in favour of the Constitution by 36% to 33%. But there was discouraging news for the yes-camp from a poll conducted for the Financial Times by the opinion pollsters, MORI, in April 2005. They concentrated on the views of 200 corporate financial directors, ranging from the smallest companies to the largest. They found 68% were opposed to the Constitution, and it made no difference how large their companies were. However, many said they could be persuaded to change their minds in certain conditions. MORI's chairman, Robert Worcester, argued that this could be done but only if the Constitution was presented as "a limiting, rather than an enabling Constitution". This analysis perfectly fitted the generally Euro-sceptic tone of British public opinion. As Worcester put it of the EU, "We've got them in a box they can't escape from."

He is right that the Constitution is largely unknown in Britain. Because Blair had delayed the referendum until 2006, few people, including politicians, had really focused on what the Constitution actually contained. The battle lines were not yet drawn up, except in the broadest terms. The Conservative party was against the Constitution, and promised to renegotiate it if it got back into power. The Labour party and the Liberal Democrats were in favour. The yes-camp's arguments centred on the new Charter of Human Rights, which would make rights judiciable for the first time. They pointed out that the working of the EU's institutions would be improved with a European Foreign Minister and a full-time and renewable two-term EU president instead of the rotating six-month presidencies.

The mood shifted after the French and Dutch no-votes. Suddenly the argument about the economic character of the EU became more prominent, as people realised there was a choice between the social model and the neo-liberal one. In Downing Street, Blair developed a new line on Europe. The central issue was no longer political integration, but the union's economic orientation. Was it to be a forward-looking meritocracy run on neo-liberal lines with internal labour market flexibility and the aim of reducing trade barriers to the rest of the world or was it to be an inward-looking union which tried to retain its social model and protectionism in the face of global challenges? With Britain preparing to assume the EU presidency, he also put the whole issue of budgetary reform on the table and claimed to speak for the EU's ten new members. This fitted in with the traditional British strategy of emphasising widening rather than deepening. In as much as the collapse of the Constitution was a defeat for the integrationists, Blair saw no tragedy in it.

Ireland

Ireland is one of the member countries that have held the most referendums on European integration. In all the treaty debates, the primary points in dispute have been sovereignty, neutrality, defence and the question about whether European legislation is above national legislation. The general perception is that 80% of all Irish legislation comes from Brussels, but if you look closer at the political topics that preoccupy the Irish, domestic politics dominate. It was not until France and the Netherlands voted 'no' that Ireland started debating EU questions and, contrary to many other member countries, it is the EU's role regarding globalisation that especially concerns the Irish people.

Many Referendums, But No Debate

by Alan Dukes

Alan Dukes is the Director General of the Irish Institute of European Affairs.

Ireland is one of the countries that have held the most referendums on issues of European integration. The 1970 referendum on accession to the then EEC was followed by referendums on the Single European Act and on the Maastricht, the Amsterdam, and (twice) the Nice Treaties. The reason for this lies in the Irish Constitution and in the jurisprudence of the Irish Supreme Court.

The Irish Constitution can be amended only by referendum of the electorate. It follows that any European Treaty amendment that impinges on the Constitution can be implemented in Ireland only if it has been assented to in a referendum.

In 1986, the Irish government considered that the Single European Act did not impinge on the Constitution and could therefore be ratified by the Oireachtas (the bicameral parliament). This view was challenged and the Supreme Court ruled that a referendum was required. Ever since, the view has been taken that a referendum should be held on each European treaty amendment, even where, as in the case of the Amsterdam Treaty, there is an arguable case that it does not impinge on the Constitution.

In every European referendum debate since 1987, it has been suggested by the media that insufficient information was given to the public. This suggestion has featured even in those media organs, which devoted a considerable amount of attention to reports on proceedings at the intergovernmental conferences (IGCs). There was rarely any comment about the fact that these formally secret proceedings generally proved to be more accessible to the media than the internal policy discussions of national governments.

The Convention on the Future of Europe attracted considerable media attention. The then Minister of State for European Affairs took a high profile part in the proceedings and was closely and publicly identified with moves by the smaller Member States to assert their right to full consideration of their interests. Irish members of the Convention, like their counterparts from other Member States, consulted extensively with their political parties and with a wide range of interest groups. Much of this activity received media attention.

After the rejection of the Nice Treaty in the 2001 referendum, the Irish government set up the National Forum on Europe to promote and facilitate wide-ranging debate on EU issues. The forum includes members of all political parties represented in the Oireachtas and non-party representatives. It also has an Observer Pillar, which includes representatives of all the recognised Social Partners and of other civil society groups. It holds regular plenary sessions, usually addressed by prominent personalities who then engage in debate with members and observers. It also holds special public sessions in regional centres throughout the country, to give the general public greater access to debate on European issues. Many of these public sessions (particularly those held between the 2001 and the 2002 referendums) have been very well attended: others have had only sparse attendance.

For the 2001 and 2002 referendums on the Nice Treaty, the government set up a Referendum Commission, charged with providing information to the public on the cases being made by both pro- and anti-ratification groups. The Referendum Commission does not take a position on any of the issues in debate: it simply reports to the public on positions being propounded by groups active in the debate, using print, broadcast and electronic media. The experience has been mixed. Members of the public have reported that they have felt confused by reading a Referendum Commission document that presents diametrically opposed views on a given issue on adjoining pages.

The evidence from opinion polls suggests that this extensive and unprecedented activity and coverage has so far impacted mainly on those with an active interest in EU issues, and did not penetrate very far into the general public consciousness.

Similarly, decisions by eleven Member States to ratify the treaty (including the Spanish referendum decision) have made far less impact on public opinion than the French and Dutch referendum rejections.

The implications of the French and Dutch rejections have not yet been absorbed. There is a clear difficulty in analysing the meaning of such a rejection, a difficulty that arose in Ireland following the rejection of the Nice Treaty in 2001. In each case, it can be surmised that the no-votes were motivated by a range of different, and often conflicting, considerations, and this creates clear difficulties in defining an appropriate response. There are clearly a variety of possible responses, each of which will have a differential effect on contrasting segments of both the 'no' and the yes-voters.

Polling analysis following the two Nice Treaty referendums in Ireland suggested that:

- the motivations of no-voters on each occasion were varied and, to a significant extent, mutually contradictory,
- the no-voters on each occasion were broadly the same people but that, on the second occasion, people who thought that the referendum was bound to pass on the first occasion and therefore did not vote came out to vote on the second occasion,
- no-voters are, in general, more strongly motivated than yes-voters.

There is no evidence that would allow any conclusion to be drawn as to the effect of the further protective provision in relation to Irish participation in military activities, which the government added to the referendum question for the second Nice referendum in 2002.

These considerations raise clear questions about the suitability of the referendum method for making decisions on multi-faceted proposals (as opposed to what might be termed 'single-issue' proposals).

Sovereignty and the supremacy of EU law over national law have been key issues in every Irish debate on an EU Treaty. In the immediate aftermath of the June 2004 European Council, the claim by a former Irish MEP that the constitutional treaty contained, allegedly for the first time, a provision to the effect that the proposed EU Constitution and laws would prevail over the Irish Constitution and laws created something of a stir. This was despite the fact that this had been the case for over thirty years in those policy areas where the Member States have agreed, in previous treaties, to confer competence on the EU.

It seems clear that references to an EU 'Constitution' provoke adverse reactions in some sections of Irish (as well as French and Dutch) public opinion. It is clear also that Irish public opinion is either unaware of or unimpressed by statements by the European Court of Justice to the effect that the treaties, in some parts, have "the character of a Constitution".

The constitutional treaty proposals to expand the number of policy areas in which decisions would be made by qualified majority voting are seen in some circles as a further cession of national sovereignty rather than as the intended facilitation of efficiency in decision-making.

There is a popular perception that "80% of Irish legislation originates in Brussels". While this may very well be correct when referring to the volume of legislation passed, it is also the case that nothing like 80% of public debate on 'hot' political topics is devoted to legislation on EU issues, but focuses instead on issues of purely national competence.

Until 2003, scrutiny of EU legislative proposals by the Oireachtas was not very thorough. In the light of experience with the two referendums on the Nice Treaty, the government sponsored new arrangements to increase the amount of parliamentary attention devoted to this area. The experience so far appears positive at parliamentary level. It remains to be seen, however, whether this has any noticeable impact on public opinion or on the general level of public understanding of EU issues.

Neutrality and defence have figured as issues of contention in every public debate on EU Treaty amendments in Ireland. The evidence suggests that Irish people generally take a good deal of pride in their country's participation in UN peacekeeping operations. It is held that Ireland's neutrality (or non-involvement in military alliances) makes Irish troops particularly acceptable participants in such operations. The implicit corollary – that troops from NATO Member States or from States engaged in other military alliances are less acceptable – is rarely subjected to any systematic analysis. Moves by the EU to develop actions with any military connotation are seen, by some sections of the Irish public, as creating the danger of drawing Ireland closer to NATO. It is for this reason that the 2002 referendum question on the Nice Treaty added a new restriction in the Irish Constitution to the government's powers and those of the Oireachtas to engage in military commitments outside of specific UN mandates.

There are indications that, on this occasion, the debate on these issues may be less heated. The allegation that the EU is somehow becoming a 'military club' with imperialistic ambitions appears to have lost much of its force following the divisions that emerged over the US-UK invasion of Iraq.

The 2004 enlargement seems to have been accepted without great difficulty by Irish public opinion. The hosting of the 'Day of Welcomes' on 1 May by the Irish Prime Minister and President struck a powerful note of resonance with the Irish population at large.

In the year following the May 2004 enlargement, some 60,000 nationals of the new Member States registered with the Irish Social Security authorities. That would be the equivalent of about 800,000 persons registering in the UK or France. This inflow (clearly affected by Ireland's waiving of the restrictions allowed by the Accession Treaties) has been absorbed without difficulty, largely because there is a state of virtually full employment in Ireland.

While the 2004 enlargement poses no apparent difficulties in Ireland and there is a general expectation that Bulgaria and Romania will join in due course, there is some uncertainty about attitudes to possible future enlargements. Turkey has so far figured very little in public debate. Whether this reflects an open-minded attitude or a reluctance to express opinions, which might be characterised as religiously intolerant, remains to be seen. Croatia sparks little attention: this probably reflects a generally positive attitude. There is, however, clear unease about the other States of the former Yugoslavia and about Albania, Ukraine, Belarus and Moldova. References to the countries of the Caucasus give rise, in general, to outright bafflement.

Despite the situation of virtually full employment in Ireland, the complex of issues described as 'globalisation' gives rise to considerable public concern. The Sapir report (2003), the Kok report (2004) and the Lisbon Agenda mean nothing to the general public, even though the issues addressed are matters of urgent public concern. There is no clear perception in the public mind that the EU plays an immediate or useful role in dealing with these concerns.

Nor is there any general public appreciation of the fact that the EU, as the world's largest trading entity, benefits from globalisation by having increasing market access for its products and services. This can be seen as odd in a country that has one of the most open economies in the EU, a country that would be unable to support its current high per capita income levels if it were not a relatively large net exporter.

The EU's performance in the area of economic policy coordination and in the enforcement of fiscal discipline is another area in which it has acquired a negative image in Irish public opinion. There is a perception that 'small' Member States (Ireland, Portugal and the Netherlands) have been more severely treated for lesser lapses then 'big' Member States (France, Germany and Italy). The Commission's strictures on Irish fiscal policy in 2002 are seen as largely egregious in the light of Ireland's subsequent performance and of the way in which both the Commission and the Council were seen to have 'given in' to France and Germany in particular.

The constitutional treaty proposals in relation to economic policy coordination have not generally been seen as a major advance in this area. Neither has the EU's performance to date on achieving the Lisbon Agenda targets been such as to inspire confidence in its ability to contribute significantly to re-launching economic growth.

Last June's European Council decided to allow a period of reflection of one year before returning to the constitutional treaty. It is now clear that a substantial part of that reflection should be devoted to explaining, in a way that will attract public attention and understanding, what the EU actually does and how that affects the well-being of its citizens. No debate about the future can make much sense if it is not based on an accurate grasp of the present.

Portugal

Portugal is traditionally one of the most positive EU countries. This is partly because the EU helps to secure democracy and a reasonable relationship with the ever-present big brother Spain, and partly because the EU is a wellspring of economic incentives. However, since the French and the Dutch 'no', the enthusiasm has been on the decline. The debate about the constitutional treaty revealed that the population has only a scant knowledge of the EU, and the debate is marked by the country's economic stagnation and rising unemployment that, in conjunction with the French and Dutch 'no', have made the population more sceptical. The relationship between the large and small countries in the EU is one of the most sensitive topics in Portugal, which fears that the continued enlargements will lead to less influence for the small countries.

A Small Country Seeking Security And Influence

by Teresa de Sousa (translated by Bettina Myers)

Teresa de Sousa is a columnist of the Portuguese daily newspaper PÚBLICO and a European and International Affairs analyst. She writes for a number of Portuguese and international journals specialising in international politics and European affairs, and teaches in a Lisbon university.

The debate on the European Constitution in Portugal has coincided with persistent economic stagnation, which has meant increased unemployment and a permanent crisis that have been attenuated, but not eliminated, by the general elections of 20 February 2005. Though Portugal is traditionally a 'Euro-enthusiast', this feeling of crisis is a factor of unpredictability that might have affected the result of the referendum, initially planned for October at the same time as the local elections but now postponed until a better moment. Like most of the countries in the Union that had also planned referendums, the Portuguese government accepted the decision of the European Council, meeting in Brussels on 16 and 17 June, to suspend the process for a year. The effect of the double rejection by both France and the Netherlands has also been felt keenly in Portugal. An opinion poll carried out two weeks after the French referendum indicated a sharp increase in the no-camp, putting favourable and unfavourable opinions on the same level for the first time.

One of the main issues in the campaign for this year's general elections was precisely the fact that, for the first time since Portugal joined the EEC, the country is diverging from the average level of affluence in Europe, after over fifteen years of accelerated convergence. The idea that we are already about to be overtaken by newcomers to the Union from Eastern Europe, has contributed to the crisis of confidence in the country's future within the European framework.

At the same time, national concerns about the public debt and stagnating growth are so serious that the debate on the Constitution has been relegated to a real second place. It is this lack of interest that explains the decision of the government to have called the referendum for the same day as the local elections, with the support of the largest opposition party, in an attempt to prevent the risk of a very high abstention rate. In the elections for the European Parliament in June 2004, Portugal recorded an abstention rate of 61%, which was exceptionally high, particularly when compared to the countries of 'old' Europe.

Portugal has never consulted the public about participation in the EU. It did not do so when it joined what was then the EEC on 1 January 1986, nor later when the Maastricht Treaty was ratified. The Portuguese Constitution itself did not authorise referendums for international treaties and, for that reason, had to be changed. Many people still believe that a parliamentary vote would be enough to approve the Constitution. But pressure has been stronger from the defenders of the 'no' who hope to succeed in preventing its ratification, and from some of the more pro-European public figures who think that the country's preference for Europe should be legitimised.

So far there has been little debate on the constitutional treaty (it was more intense when the Convention was taking place), and it has been almost completely limited to the voices arguing for 'no'. The problem is that in every opinion poll the Portuguese have shown little knowledge of the Constitution's content. Portuguese public opinion follows the vicissitudes of the referendums in other countries with a certain distance, though the elite and the quality newspapers pay a great deal of attention to what is happening in France.

The two no-results in two founding countries of the European Union have intensified the debate, particularly in the media, giving a new 'impulse' to the public figures who oppose the constitutional treaty. On the yes-side, hesitation and contradiction have prevailed about what to do from now on: whether to hold the referendum, for example.

In short, it can be said today that the traditional 'Euro-enthusiasm' of the Portuguese people is in a phase of apathy that the defenders of the 'no' may well use to their advantage, as they have done in other European countries.

The latest extensive Eurobarometer survey of knowledge and acceptance of the Constitution in the 25 Member States (conducted in the autumn of 2004 and published in 2005) shows some worrying signs. Asked about their knowledge of the Constitution, 39% of Portuguese people said they knew nothing about its content, 50% per cent said they knew about it vaguely and only 11% said they knew it well or very well. Asked about their support of the Constitution, though only 7% rejected the new treaty, only 40% said they supported it, and over 50% were indifferent. Of course, answers vary a great deal according to the level of education and income; the lower the level of education and income, the less knowledge and more opposition to the new treaty. A study conducted for the Commission in Portugal by the ICS (Institute of Social Sciences), using data from the Eurobarometer, found, for example, that the percentage of respondents with confidence in the European Union is very high among certain groups in the population: younger people (74%), people with more education (78%) and those who feel well informed about Europe (89%).

Even without the prospect of an imminent referendum, there is no strong trend towards Euro-scepticism or anti-Europeanism in Portugal, and no guarantee that consulting the public about the constitutional treaty would bring a negative result, even under the present circumstances. Firstly, the major Portuguese political parties, the PS on the centre-left and the PSD on the centre-right, represented almost 75% of the votes in the elections and both are firmly in favour of Europe and the European Constitution.

Secondly, the PS, the most pro-European party on the Portuguese political scene, came to government with a comfortable majority in parliament and a great deal of public confidence in its favour.

But some parties on the margins of the party system ferociously oppose the Constitution, and, even more serious than that, there is a group of very prominent intellectual and academic figures (particularly on the centre-right) who have already begun to campaign against the constitutional treaty. There are differences between the left and the right in the smaller parties. On the left, the old Communist Party (perhaps the only Communist party in Western Europe which has not been able to achieve its 'aggiornamento' since the fall of the Berlin Wall) is against the Constitution, just as it has been against all the previous European treaties. It declares itself to be against "capitalist Europe" and fights tooth and nail to defend "national sovereignty". The second party to the left of the PS – the 'Left-wing Block', which unites Marxists, *altermundialistas* and environmentalists – also argues for a rejection, though with other arguments which come closer to the left-wing defenders of the French 'no'.

Lastly, there is the Partido Popular, to the right of the party spectrum, which has already changed its characteristics and position on Europe several times. It began as a small Christian-Democratic party, which was very much in favour of European integration. Then it went through a phase of anti-European nationalism. This was followed by its transformation into a populist, right-wing, 'Euro-resistant' party, before it arrived at the current new phase in its evolution (following the fall of the coalition government that it had formed with the PSD until last February), which is a little more favourable towards the Constitution.

As well as its similarities to other countries, the Portuguese debate has also been different in certain aspects. Curiously enough, some academics and intellectuals decided to make a hobbyhorse out of the article in the new treaty establishing the subordination of national constitutional law to the European Constitution, considering it inadmissible. The subordination of national laws to those of the Community is a long-established fact that has never been questioned in Portugal. In a country with eight centuries of history, this argument revives the old spectre of the country's loss of sovereignty, which was important during the initial phase of the European debate in Portugal. Now it is given a new and more 'threatening' context: a Europe expanded to include 25 Member States in which a small, peripheral nation will be destined to lose its identity and influence on European decision-making.

It has to be understood that the traditional Portuguese right-wing Euro-sceptics have never expressed their opposition to the European Union. On the contrary, they spend their lives affirming their Europeanism. They say that the construction of Europe is happening too quickly, that public opinion in most countries does not understand this haste, and that it should be halted. They defend the model of the 'Europe of nation-states' against a hybrid supranational construction 'subordinated to the Franco-German directorate' and to the 'bureaucracy of Brussels', whose power they accuse of continuously growing. On the political left, the Communists and the left-wing block prefer to use the closure of companies, which have transferred to Slovakia or Romania, or of the 'impositions' of the Stability and Growth Pact (SGP), to accuse Europe of not serving the interests of the workers and the country in general.

But despite the negative circumstances under which the referendum was to be have been held, it must be remembered that Portugal has been a 'Euro-enthusiast' almost from the moment it joined the EU in 1986, for reasons which have evolved with time, but which continue to have a great influence on Portuguese public opinion. The initial motivation for Portugal's accession to, what was at that time, the European Community, was political – very similar in fact to what led the post-Communist countries of Central and Eastern Europe to ask for their 'return to Europe' as soon as they freed themselves from Soviet domination. Portugal sought to consolidate the democracy it had won back in April 1974 after a long dictatorship, and to make it irreversible with permanent integration in Western democracy. In Portugal, the first European banner was also the 'return to Europe', from which we had been kept away by the longest European dictatorship of the 20th century (though blander than the others were) and to the African military adventure of almost 15 years (from 1961 to 1974) to preserve the colonial empire.

There were also economic motivations. Lagging behind Europe, Portugal had to speed up its economic development and saw European integration as a vital springboard for achieving this. As soon as Portugal joined the EU, economic reasons became increasingly important. The idea progressively gained ground in Portuguese public opinion that Europe meant Community funds. The 'money from Brussels' started to take over completely and the Community was seen as a continuous source of financial transfers, which would mean rapid economic development and a better life for the population.

Europe has never won so much approval in Portugal as in this long period of accelerated economic convergence, which lasted right up until its entry into the euro in 1999. The Portuguese also began to share a feeling of (sometimes ambivalent) pride about belonging to a 'club of the wealthy'. Eduardo Lourenço, Portugal's most distinguished essayist, describes this ambivalence as "this curious way of 'separating ourselves' from Europe or of thinking that the real Europe is separate from us", which is expressed by the "old distinction between the Europe on the other side and the Europe on this side of the Pyrenees". Catching up with the others, said Lourenço, is "becoming part of the real Europe".

For the first few years, the idea of Europe as a springboard for economic and social modernism also predominated among the elite. The centre-right government (PSD) headed by Cavaco Silva, who led the country from accession until 1995, had a vision of European integration which was more economic and less political, unlike the socialists of Mário Soares (who worked so much for Portugal's European preference). During the negotiations for the Maastricht Treaty, Cavaco Silva distrusted the new political dimension of European construction, though he had been quick to support the objective of the economic and monetary union. During this phase, Portuguese diplomacy still followed the British position more easily than the Paris-Bonn axis (the United Kingdom is Portugal's oldest ally).

It was from 1992, the year of Portugal's first Presidency of the European Union that this 'economic' vision of European integration began to give way to one that was globally more political. During those six months of Lisbon's presidency, the Portuguese saw themselves as 'real Europeans' for the first time. But it was the arrival of António Guterres' PS to government in 1995 which marked a turning point in Portugal's European politics. From then on, the idea that 'Portugal always has to be at the centre of European construction' began to dominate Lisbon's behaviour in Brussels. 'Being at the centre of Europe' is the only way to change Portugal's peripheral position and to combat its geographical, historical and economic marginality. Being at the centre of Europe began to mean that the country had to be part of the most advanced group for European integration, be it for the euro, the Schengen agreement, or European defence.

The country finally gained European maturity with Guterres and Portugal's accession to the euro. In March 2000, during Portugal's second presidency of the EU, it was at the initiative of the António Guterres government that the European Council approved the Lisbon Strategy. Portugal was able to free itself from the image of a country 'with its hand out' for funds and to assume the status of a country which also feels responsible for Europe's destiny. Europe was no longer just a case of structural funds. The perception of the elite was that Portugal's participation in the EU had greatly improved the country's international status and was a vital asset for the defence of our national interests. But the public still has the idea that this is a poor country with little ability to make itself heard in Brussels, and one that still needs funds from Brussels. This perception has been accentuated by the last enlargement, seen by both public opinion and some of the elite, as a threat to financial aid and to the influence of Portugal in the European Union.

The nationalist anti-European tendency has gradually lost its influence with the success of Portugal's European integration. Rare are the voices today which are against Portugal staying in the European Union or which assume the same attitudes as Jean-Marie Le Pen in France. Everyone says they are 'for Europe'. The problem only starts when they discuss what sort of Europe is in Portugal's best interest. Most of the political elite follow the trend of the so-called 'Confirmed Europeans', though very few Portuguese public figures openly declare themselves to be federalists. Mário Soares, still a well-respected figure in politics, is in this camp. But then so is the current minister of foreign affairs, Diogo Freitas do Amaral, who was leader of a small Democratic Christian party during the first few years of democracy.

This lack of enthusiasm about federalism (the word 'federal' has almost always been banished from political arguments) has to do with Portugal's self-image. On the one hand, there is a strong national identity (the nation has eight centuries of history that the Portuguese tend to imagine as glorious); and on the other, is a certain inferiority complex, common with a small, poor and peripheral country. An understanding of the most important issues, which have permeated the European debate in Portugal, must begin with the country's geopolitical situation at the westernmost point of Europe, and with its historically marginal position held throughout most of the 20th century. It is this historical and geographical influence that often causes a defensive attitude towards new advances in the construction of Europe, which is expressed even in the most pro-European camp.

There are four main issues in this debate, interpreted according to the circumstances of the construction of Europe through time:
- marginality and centrality
- relationship between 'big' and 'small' countries
- economic and social cohesion
- European vocation versus Atlantic vocation.

From the moment Portugal opted strategically for Europe, just three years after the revolution of 25 April 1974, the issue of marginality was only raised as a risk to be combated. The possibility of finding an alternative to Europe in the South Atlantic (in Portuguese-speaking Africa and Brazil) was hardly considered at all from 1986 onwards.

As I have already said, political centrality in the EU gained enormous importance in European decisions from 1995, when Lisbon progressively abandoned the role of 'good European pupil' with its hand held out for structural funds and began to see itself as a European country involved in all EU decisions. This explains Lisbon's determination to be in the euro. And this explains why, from 1995 onwards, Portugal was in all of the EU's and NATO's peace missions in the Balkans.

But, on the other hand, the relationship between the 'big' and the 'small' is perhaps the most sensitive issue. During negotiations for the Nice Treaty, the Portuguese debate was polarised around the risk of a 'directory' of big countries. This fear continues to be felt, both in public opinion and among the elite. This perception explains the almost obsessive way that the Portuguese representatives in the Convention have defended the principle of equality between the Member States; or the attachment to the idea of one commissioner per Member State; or even the great difficulty with which Lisbon has accepted the proposal, officially part of the Constitution today, of a president of the European Council substituting the six-month rotation of presidencies. In 2000, an opinion poll conducted in Portugal showed that the Portuguese people considered that the most negative aspect of joining the EU was the fact that the 'small' depended on the decisions of the 'big'. This will be one of the main arguments of the no-camp.

The debate's third point of economic and social cohesion is practically consensual. Through time, it has meant an overvaluation of financial aid from Brussels as 'almost' the only subject in the European debate. Only today, when enlargement involves the transfer of aid from the countries of the South to the countries of the East, are there people who are brave enough to publicly argue for an end to the Brussels' 'subsidy dependence'. But extorting support from Brussels continues to be a kind of duty for any Portuguese government and a measure of its European success or failure.

Finally, there is the old issue of conciliation between the European and the Atlantic vocations of Portuguese foreign policy. Before accession to the EU, the debate was centred on those who argued for our 'return to Europe' as a fundamental strategic preference, and those who continued to argue in favour of the predominance of our relationship with Africa and Brazil in continuation from the old regime. The latter trend, which rapidly dissipated, chose Spain and the European continent as our main 'enemy' – near and far.

If we seek a good understanding of Portugal's preference for Europe, we have to begin by understanding the 800-year long tempestuous relationship with our great Iberian neighbour. Portugal only has one land border – with Spain, which is the oldest and most stable border in Europe – and its history is entwined with the fight to maintain its independence from Madrid. Through the centuries, it was the Atlantic 'border' that gave Portugal a strategic space, which allowed the country to sustain this historical aberration, one that even Catalunya was unable to preserve. The two Iberian countries underwent democratic revolutions almost simultaneously, in 1974 and 1975. Democracy led to a sharing of the same international alliances – the EU and NATO – for the first time in their history. This also represented a great 'revolution' in national political mentalities and perceptions. Portugal's fear of Spain is much more persistent than its fear of Europe – the EU was actually seen as a more favourable framework for the new relationship between the two countries. Even today, when Iberian relations are very close from every point of view – economic, political, cultural and social – the fear of losing our independence now through Spanish economic domination is a recurring theme in the Portuguese debate.

The Maastricht Treaty and the new Common Foreign and Security Policy (CFSP), have brought the issue of the Atlantic calling versus the European calling back to the fore. For some of the elite (and also Portuguese diplomacy), the CFSP could jeopardise Portugal's relations with the world outside Europe, particularly with Africa, Brazil and the United States. Portugal's active participation in missions to Bosnia and Kosovo, and above all the European support for the independence of East Timor in 1999, helped to consolidate the idea that "national security is defended in Bosnia" (and not in Angola), in the words of the current president of the Commission, José Manuel Durão Barroso, as head of Portuguese diplomacy in 1994.

The European experience eventually reconciled the two European and Atlantic areas of Portuguese foreign policy, which were seen as complementary rather than antagonistic, and no longer a problem. The issue only re-emerged with the Iraq crisis, which, for the first time since Portugal joined the EU, broke the great national consensus between the two main parties on foreign policy. The government at the time, headed by the leader of the centre-right party, Durão Barroso, went along with the United States and the United Kingdom, arguing that the safeguard of the transatlantic relationship was at stake. The PS, still in opposition, openly opposed the war and the decision of the government. The tension created by this division has been largely overcome today. But Portugal prefers a Europe as an ally of the United States and fears, more than anything, a Europe as a rival to the USA, which would put the Euro-Atlantic dimension of its foreign policy under great pressure. The right-wing Euro-sceptics are sure to use this 'sensitive cord' to oppose the new European minister of foreign affairs and the new European diplomatic service foreseen in the Constitution.

How are these major trends in public opinion being expressed today in the debate on the European Constitution? The opinion polls all continue to indicate that the majority of Portuguese people are in favour of the EU, though there has been a slight, but continuous change in the other direction. The same happens with the Constitution, though the 'indifference party' is in the majority. The major parties are committed to 'yes', as are the most respected political figures: Mário Soares, the father of Portuguese democracy and former President of the Republic; Cavaco Silva and António Guterres, former prime ministers of the PSD and PS; António Vitorino, the former Portuguese commissioner and one of the country's most popular figures, and the President of the European Commission and former prime minister, José Manuel Durão Barroso. The Portuguese president, Jorge Sampaio, has been telling the nation about Europe and the Constitution at every opportunity.

With or without the referendum, the European debate will continue in Portugal, but now it will continue within the framework of the deep crisis in the European Union, which the Brussels summit served to worsen rather than help dissipate. Portugal is still very sensitive to the issue of economic and social cohesion. The debate will be conditioned by the failure of negotiations for a multi-annual budget, which would have been very satisfactory for Portugal, and the fear that it will be more difficult to guarantee the same advantages in the future. The no-camp will exploit the double failure in Brussels.

Furthermore, the issue of the 'directory' of the big countries was and will be one of the central arguments against the European Constitution. The fear of an expanded Europe, responsible for the relocation of the multinationals and unemployment, and for Portugal's loss of influence in the European bodies, is another argument.

The risk is that the crisis of confidence experienced by the country may make Europe the main scapegoat. The perspective of reduced funds from the Community – the money from Brussels once again – and the people's great ignorance of what the new constitutional treaty actually says and what it is for, will make a battle for 'yes' very difficult – perhaps more difficult than the polls are showing today.

Spain

There has never been any EU resistance to speak of amongst the Spanish population. Since the end of Franco's dictatorship, the EU has been one of the main reasons for the economic growth and democratic development that has occurred in Spain. There was almost no debate about the constitutional treaty, and about 77% of the population voted 'yes' in the referendum – a situation reminiscent of Spain's accession to the European Union. The Spaniard's position regarding the EU can be summed up in the motto, "What is good for Europe is good for Spain", and, contrary to many other Member States, they have no concerns about surrender of sovereignty. However, after the French and Dutch no-votes, there are signs of a developing scepticism in Spain.

Spain Is The Problem – Europe The Solution

by Andrés Ortega

Andrés Ortega is editor of the Spanish Edition of Foreign Policy Magazine and editorial writer and columnist for El País, Spain's major newspaper.

Spain was the first country to have a referendum on the European Constitution. On 20 February 2005, the yes-vote won by a clear majority with a sufficient participation. No surprise there. After the French and Dutch referendums, Prime Minister José Luis Rodríguez Zapatero became the most ardent supporter of continuing the process of ratification in the remaining countries. However, he was unwilling to offer any alternative, and unable to get any political rent in the EU of the Spanish behaviour.

European identity is now obviously a part of Spanish identity. "Spain is the problem and Europe the solution," wrote the Spanish philosopher, José Ortega y Gasset, in 1910. And he was clearly right. Spain's recent history, its transition from Franco's dictatorship to full democracy and its process of political, economic and cultural modernisation, cannot be understood without a reference to Europe. Being able to join what is now the European Union was a major tool for modernisation and democratisation. It has also provided a framework to manage the devolution of power to the regions, the

Autonomous Communities, especially the most historical ones and where local nationalism was stronger, for example Catalonia and the Basque Country. Given the pacifist streak present in Spanish public opinion, there has also been some resistance to the idea of the EU becoming a 'superpower' or a 'military power', but that was not debated in any depth during the campaign for the referendum.

So, the vote took place last February with a very strong support, but also a strong public ignorance on the Constitution in spite of the effort made by the government to inform the Spanish people. The Accession Treaty, signed just 20 years ago on 12 June 1985, was ratified unanimously in parliament. No referendum, no great debate. It was part of the national consensus and it fulfilled an aspiration of the democratic forces in Spain. As had been promised by Felipe González during his successful campaign in 1982, there was a referendum on NATO membership at the beginning of 1986, once Spain was securely in the European Community, on whether to stay in NATO which Spain had joined in June 1982, some months after a failed coup d'état. It was won by the government, in a paradoxical setting: the main opposition party, the centre-right Popular Party (PP) who was in favour of membership, abstained, thinking the vote would be lost and González would then have to resign. By then the vote had become a kind of plebiscite on Felipe González. And he won.[10] In 2005, again in opposition, the PP did not commit the same mistake.

From 1985, Spain had made a great effort to adapt itself to the new competition and rules in the EU. Before concluding this adaptation, it had to make a supplementary effort for the Single Act and the single internal market. But joining brought a great economic bonanza until 1992. Then it had to stretch itself to join the European Monetary Union and the euro, again with no discussion and several devaluations of the peseta, some of them justified and some not, so great was the consensus. In opposition at the time, the PP had not been too keen, but once in government in 1996, José María Aznar saw it as the major tool to bring macroeconomics in line, and Spain finally joined the single currency in 1999, along with the rest of the willing Member States.

Spain's history in the EU has been a success, helped by the transfer of funds from Brussels, which amounted to over 1% of Spanish GDP, and also the building of the Spanish democracy, which coincided with the major development of the EU. Sharing sovereignty is not a problem for a Spain that has become one of the most decentralised states in the Union. But Aznar's government changed some things, mainly taking sides with Britain,

---

[10] With a participation of 59.43%, against 75.11% in the referendum on the Spanish Constitution of 1978.

away from the traditional friendship with France and Germany, on political and economic issues. Aznar supported the US and British positions towards the invasion of Iraq and contributed to the division of what Donald Rumsfeld termed the 'old' and the 'new' Europe. In socioeconomic terms, Aznar also favoured a more Anglo-Saxon model rather than the Renanian one of France and Germany but the polls showed that Spaniards considered France and Germany to be the best allies of Europe. All that without an explanation to a public opinion fiercely opposed – by over 80%, including many voters of the Popular Party – to the war in Iraq, when the small participation in the Gulf war of 1991 against the invasion of Kuwait by Iraq was broadly supported, because it was done under a European framework or umbrella. And then the 11 March bombing in Madrid; it was the way Aznar handled the situation and the information – insisting on the ETA link – that contributed to the defeat of the PP three days later in the general elections.

Zapatero's arrival as prime minister brought a change in outlook towards Europe with a re-rapprochement to France and Germany. In the European Council in December 2003, Aznar had blocked the European Constitution on the grounds that, compared to the Nice Treaty, Spain lost institutional power (mainly in the voting system in the Council), but Zapatero accepted the solution that was on the table of a mixed system of states and populations, in a Constitution, 90% of which had been negotiated by Aznar's government with the support of the socialists in the Convention and afterwards.

It is in this setting that the referendum on the European Constitution was called. Some months before, thinking that the Constitution would be ready for the European elections of June 2004, the Spanish parliament had approved, almost by unanimity, to call the referendum on the European Constitution. The PP was not so keen anymore on the referendum. It would have preferred to have had it at a later date, perhaps September 2005, and with more time to campaign. But Zapatero's government thought it advantageous for Spain to be the first country to approve the Constitution by referendum. (Even if the referendum was only consultative, the government had stated that it would reject the text if the 'no' triumphed). To have been the fourth, fifth, or seventh would have put Spain in an unnoticeable position. To be the first meant sending a signal, not just to the Spaniards but also to others, including the French. Chirac and Schröder campaigned in Spain and, in return, Zapatero campaigned in France in socialist meetings. The rejection of the treaty in the referendums in France, (described in the first instance by the Spanish government as a 'stumble') and then Holland, (they then elevated the rejection to the category of 'added difficulty', and finally used the word 'crisis') had the government starting to gauge that the Constitution would never be ratified, although it favoured the continuation of the ratification process. This does not necessarily put Spain in a bad position. It shows that the worrying distance between the political class and the citizens in those countries does not apply to Spain, perhaps because the change of government has been very recent: a prelude to the change of generation in power in Europe in the years to come, but it did not bring any advantages for Spain in the negotiation of the financial perspectives for 2007-2013 in the sad European Council in Brussels in June. The Popular Party has, again, tried to push its different vision of Europe, distancing itself from the Constitution after the French and Dutch referendums, and asking Zapatero to cut ties with the Franco-German partnership, called by the PP leader, Mariano Rajoy, "the axis of the losers". Zapatero did not use the Spanish advantage to push for new ideas. Maybe the crisis came upon him too soon, scarcely a year after having formed his government.

The socialists, for who "more Europe" has always been part of their ideological identity, had launched themselves in a very active, but short, campaign for the referendum. The PP did as well, although less actively, as it thought Spain had loss institutional weight in the final negotiation of the Constitution, a feeling not shared by the majority of public opinion. There is more than a suspicion that it also pushed for other options on the side. The fact that in some upper class areas in Madrid the 'no' prevailed tends to confirm the suspicion that they supported the Treaty only half-heartedly when they did not decide for an outright rejection. They went for a 'yes, but with reservations'.

The Izquierda Unida, a coalition group based around the Communist party, and the left nationalists in Catalonia and the Basque Country went openly for the 'no'. The antiglobalisation movements, very strong in Catalonia, also went for the 'no'. Izquierda Unida campaigned on social issues but accused the Constitution of bringing back the possibility of the death penalty, hindering the right to strike, or supporting "pre-emptive wars", which clearly were a manipulation of the text. The moderate or centre-right nationalists in both regions had a very strong internal debate on what position to take, mainly because the Constitution set the "union of states and citizens", against the "union of peoples" (relegated to the Charter on Fundamental Rights) and the territorial integrity of its Member States. But finally, they pushed for a 'yes but with reservations', that is, agreeing broadly with the text but lamenting the fact that the Constitution did not assume their nationalists' vindications sufficiently. But Europe was part of their ideological background, always thinking that more Europe meant less Spain. They could not say 'no'. In the end, there was some left-right division on the Constitution, and between nationalists and non-nationalists, but it did not run too deeply.

Participation in the referendum was more than expected but less than in the European parliamentary elections of June 2004 (a dwindling participation that has shortened on each occasion). But a participation of 42.32%, given the circumstances, was more than expected and satisfactory (the PP put the minimum success at 35%), especially if coupled with a massive 'yes' of 76.73%. The no-vote came to 17.24%, mainly in the areas already mentioned (33.6% in the Basque Country and high in Navarra, and 28% in Catalonia) and the blanks, a voting option than has grown in elections in the last few years, took 6%). The young voters did not mobilise themselves, a fact that is worrying for the future of Europeanism of Spain. But this referendum also lacked internal tension, and a huge majority thought it was going to be won in any case. That was the major problem: no expectation of any surprise.

The Constitution was ratified in parliament by almost 95% of the MPs, and then in the Senate, and the Constitutional Court ruled that there was no need to adapt the Spanish Constitution to the European one. But the debate has not been very great or deep among the citizens, almost blindingly pro-European, for the reasons explained above. The majority of Spaniards approved the idea of a referendum and were in favour of a Constitution, but they did not know its content. Polls showed that 83-87% had a very low level or no knowledge of it,[11] even though the government made it very widely available to anyone interested. This was so different to France where seven books on Europe reached the bestseller lists before the referendum. But the level of approval of European integration and of the Constitution has always stayed high in Spain. Even though it was declining, it was still around 58% some weeks before the voting day.[12] And the general feeling was that what is good for Europe is good for Spain, and they thought the new constitutional treaty was good for Europe.

As for the reasons to vote[13] 'yes', the most important (38.7% in a post-referendum poll) was to continue the European construction, and this reason was defended by the political party to which the elector voted. As for the 'no', lack of information (24.5%, and 43.5% among abstainers for whom the disinterest in politics was the second reason) and insufficient social content (23%) prevailed.

The feeling of Spaniards towards Europe in an enlarged Union might change. Spain is reconciled to the perspective that less funds will come from Brussels in a Union less generous that contains more countries poorer than Spain. But if the result of the negotiation on the next Financial Perspectives (2007-2013) does not fit some of the Spanish expectations, the public

---

[11] Poll by the CIS (Centro de Investigaciones Sociológicas), December 2004, and Instituto Opina, 2 February 2005.
[12] Eurobarometer, January 2005.
[13] CIS Post-referendum Poll, February-March 2005.

opinion backlash could also be felt against the EU. Geographically, by size and by wealth, Spain is in an eccentric position. Curiously, public opinion favours the eventual entry of Russia (58%) but not so of Turkey (only 44%). However, some months earlier it had also been in favour of Turkey joining. This could become a problem. 'More Europe' is not guaranteed after the French 'non' and the Dutch 'nee,' and the virtual demise of the Constitution. Europe has become indispensable for Spain, but may not be the 'solution' to its internal problems anymore.

Finland

In spite of arguments that a referendum would lessen the growing chasm between the people and the EU, the Finnish government refrained from asking the people about the constitutional treaty. The government feared a low election turnout and an unpredictable outcome, and the inevitable result was that the growing resistance towards the EU became even more marked after the referendum in France and the Netherlands. The basic problem, according to the Finnish minister of foreign affairs, is that people are tired of the larger-than-life visions and rhetoric in the constitutional treaty. An especially sore point is the question of neutrality, which since WW2 has been an all-important dogma in Finland's foreign policy.

Referendum - Why Run The Risk?

by Nina Törnudd

Nina Törnudd covers EU affairs and politics for the Finnish News Agency in Helsinki.

One dusky, wintry afternoon in February 2005, some 50 people were sitting scattered around in the main hall of the Helsinki School of Economics. The wood-panelled hall in this 1950s building seats 600 people, but on that day looked rather empty. This was the start of a series of public debates on the European Constitution, organised by the Foreign Ministry's European Information Service. Similar events were scheduled to be held in 22 other cities around the country.

Prime Minister Matti Vanhanen addressed the meagre crowd in his habitual low-key style. He argued that the new Constitution was a significant improvement compared to the Nice Treaty: it made the union more democratic, more transparent and more efficient. And the single document was a model of clarity compared to the tangle of treaties it replaced. Vanhanen also presented his familiar argument as to why there was no need to hold a referendum in Finland.

"The Constitution does not change the European Union to the degree that a referendum would be called for," Vanhanen said. He also argued that the Constitution contained a number of things Finland had supported during previous intergovernmental conferences (IGCs), such as a deeper cooperation within justice and home affairs.

The Left Alliance MP, Outi Ojala, replied by saying that she regretted the government's decision to reject a referendum. The chasm between the people and the EU seemed only to be growing; a referendum would have been an excellent occasion to try to remedy that. Her party, together with the Greens, had been the most active proponents for holding a referendum.

When it was time for questions, few of them concerned the Constitution directly. Some of the participants had obviously been waiting for a chance to air their grievances to the prime minister.

The small but energetic anti-EU movement, Free Finland League, was represented by a man who argued that the decision to adopt the euro was contrary to the Finnish Constitution and that the euro was therefore an illegal currency. The movement had been persistently campaigning against the EU since membership began in 1995, but had never managed to win a single seat in the national or European Parliaments.

An older woman asked if the leaving out of Christianity in the Constitution meant that the EU was following the Anti-Christ. Someone raised the issue of wolves: why was Brussels stopping us from shooting wolves in rural areas, where they killed people's dogs and livestock?

Vanhanen replied as well as he could. He energetically dismissed the idea that rejecting the Constitution would allow Finland or other states to return to a system like the European Economic Area, with access to the single market but no participation in the decision-making system. He said he did not believe a single EU member would want to commit to most of the union's rules and regulations without any say in the decisions.

"Norway is in the EEA, but it is also one of the largest net contributors to the EU," Vanhanen said.

The movement for a referendum in Finland have not given up their efforts and will continue collecting signatures for its petition until the end of 2005. Some tens of thousands had been collected by spring 2005. And in parliament, a group of 50 (out of 200) members signed an initiative to hold a referendum after all.

In the end, an inner circle of the government decided the issue. Three men, Prime Minister Matti Vanhanen of the Centre Party, Finance Minister Antti Kalliomäki of the Social Democrats, and Environment Minister Jan-Erik Enestam of the Swedish People's Party, sat down together in August 2004 and decided that the government would not propose a referendum. Earlier on, the Social Democratic Party and the Centre Party had adopted the same position.

The three governing parties argued that the changes brought by the Constitution were simply not important enough to warrant a referendum. Many opponents of holding a referendum also argued that the parliament was quite capable of deciding the issue: the risk of a very low participation was significant and the result of the vote would consequently be very unpredictable. There would also be no suitable poll to combine the referendum with; the first realistic option would be the presidential elections in January 2006.

The decision not to hold a referendum on the Constitution was yet another example of the ultra-pragmatism that sometimes seems to dominate Finnish politics. While in opposition, the Centre Party had decided it would demand that a possible adhesion to NATO must be decided by referendum. But, once in government, it saw no need to consult the people on the EU Constitution.

As the idea of joining NATO was quite unpopular, it was not very likely that it would be brought up for serious discussion in the foreseeable future. Most polls showed a support of less than a third for NATO membership. The most recent poll (September/October 2004), taken by the parliamentary Advisory Board for Defence Information (MTS), showed 61% in favour of non-alignment and 34% favouring military alliance either in NATO or a militarily stronger EU. MTS polls in the past had found support for an alliance, ranging between 16 and 34%. Non-alignment had received support of between 60 and 79% in the studies that have been made twice a year since 1996.

Vanhanen's warm praise for the Constitution might have surprised some, as Finland has by no means been happy with everything that came out, first from Valéry Giscard d'Estaing's convention and then from the ensuing IGC talks on the Constitution.

Finland, among other things, had opposed the creation of European President of the Council. It also attempted, almost to the very end, to work for a division of voting power in the Council that would not favour the larger states quite as much as the final result did. Both attempts failed, but the result was qualified as a reasonable compromise all the same.

The security guarantees in paragraph 40.7 were probably the issue that made the biggest waves in Finnish discussion. Did they mean that Finland was no longer a non-aligned country? The word 'neutrality' had long since been discarded from the official phrasebook, but 'military non-alignment' remained the definition. Foreign Minister Erkki Tuomioja lobbied successfully to include a line in the Constitution stating that these guarantees did not influence any EU member's own defence arrangements.

The Constitution's most vocal Finnish critic, the Euro-sceptic MEP, Esko Seppänen, from the Left Alliance, argued that the clauses actually meant that the EU was turning into a military alliance and that Finland was being driven towards NATO membership through the back door.

The issue of non-alignment or neutrality was a sensitive one, as it had been the dominant ideal of Finnish foreign policy ever since the Second World War. Finland lost both the Winter and the Continuation War to the Soviet Union, losing a significant part of territory in the process.

Finland avoided the fate of the Baltic States who lost their independence for nearly 50 years, but had to accept a Treaty of Cooperation and Friendship with the Soviet Union. Membership in the UN, the Nordic Council, and EFTA had to be cautiously approached and membership of the EEC was seen as incompatible with neutrality. A free trade agreement with the EEC was signed in 1973, after President Urho Kekkonen managed to overcome Soviet suspicion of the move.

The gradual collapse of the Soviet Union and the migration of EFTA members to the EC changed the scene in the late 1980s. Finland saw the need for further economic integration with the European Community.

Talks on the European Economic Area took place in 1989-91. Soon afterwards Sweden surprised its neighbour by applying for full membership of the EC. Finland followed suit in spring 1992, after a winter of intense debate and discussion.

Before the application, President Mauno Koivisto never mentioned security issues as a reason for applying for membership. That this was a prime motive for him only emerged in his memoirs, published in 1995. Economic issues, integration with Finland's major trading partners and participation in European R&D programmes were presented as the motivation for seeking membership. Koivisto, ever a cautious man, did not want to take the risk that a failure to bring the process to a successful conclusion would damage the country's position at a sensitive time.

The result of the EU referendum in 1994 was by no means a foregone conclusion. The referendum itself was an unusual event, as the threshold to holding a referendum in Finland was traditionally high. Finland had held only two consultative referendums during the country's independence.

The most recent one was in October 1994, when Finns decided by a majority of 56.9% to join the European Union. The vote split the country clearly into two blocs: the cities and the South voted 'yes', the countryside said 'no'. The biggest argument on the opposing side was agriculture; it was clear that EU membership would mean major cuts in income for farmers. In consequence, only 6% of farmers voted for EU membership, 94% were against it. The typical opponent would have been a farmer with a grade school education, a below-average income, a supporter of either the Left Alliance, the Centre Party or the Christian League (now the Christian Democrats), and living in the northern part of the country.

The first referendum had decided an equally historic issue with an even larger margin. In 1931, Finns voted to do away with prohibition, by a majority of 70.6%. During its 13 years of existence, the ban on alcohol sales had led to widespread smuggling from Estonia and created a huge cottage industry of illicit stills around the country.

After these two, nothing. There was no referendum in Finland on the Amsterdam Treaty, none on joining the euro and none on the Nice Treaty. Of these, the euro issue was the most sensitive. Many voters felt they had not given their approval to doing away with the national currency, when they voted to join the EU in 1994. It was quite possible that a referendum would have rejected the idea of losing the markka.

But the government, led by Paavo Lipponen, did not want to take any chances. The bill was run through in parliament instead. Integrating Finland as deeply as possible with the EU was a main theme running during the eight years and two periods Lipponen held power.

Vanhanen, in opposition at the time, was calling for a referendum on the euro in 1997. When he came to power in June 2003, after Anneli Jäätteenmäki was forced to resign as PM, he admitted that he did not consider himself a very enthusiastic European. He did vote in favour of joining the EU after the referendum in 1994, but opposed joining the EMU.

But once in power, he came round to the same position as Lipponen, and decided against taking a risk on a popular consultation. He was helped in this by the structure of Finnish politics, where Euro-scepticism is not a political force in its own right. The need to form coalition governments means that it is very hard to get into government with a radically different EU policy.

Thus, there is no significant political party with a clear Euro-sceptic or anti-EU agenda. Only the tiny populist party, the True Finns, with three MPs and a 1.5-2% share of the vote, has adopted an anti-European and nationalist line.

Euro-scepticism in Finland is expressed through the existing parties instead – and contained in them. The Centre Party, the Left Alliance and the Christian Democrats have well known but Euro-sceptic minoritaires within their ranks but they rarely have any real influence on policy.

Of the two parties calling for a referendum on the Constitution, neither was calling for its rejection. The Greens and the Left Alliance argued their call saying that a referendum would bring the union closer to the citizen, giving rise to a real debate on the EU and its future. This would increase interest in politics and perhaps get the dismal participation in European and national elections to rise.

If the Danes, the Irish and the French got to vote, then why not us, the campaigners argued to no avail.

Vanhanen and his government held on to their plans to let parliament ratify the Constitution until the EU Summit on 16 and 17 June, when the European Council decided to shelve the ratification process for a year. The following week, the government decided to give parliament a report on the treaty instead, which allowed MPs to have a thorough discussion of the Constitution and what it would have meant for the union.

A poll published by the weekly Suomen Kuvalehti after the Summit showed that opposition to the Constitution had increased significantly after the referendums in France and the Netherlands. The poll, made by Taloustutkimus found 27% of respondents in favour of the Constitution and 29% against. Forty four percent were undecided. In April and May, support for the Constitution was 37% and only 20% were against it.

It remains to be seen if the government's information campaign and the parliamentary discussion this autumn does anything to engage Finnish voters on European issues. Abstention is a growing phenomenon in Finland. The worst result was in the European elections in 1999, when only 31.4% bothered to vote. In the next poll in 2004, the participation of 41.1% was hailed as a success. The same trend is visible in national elections, but participation has not reached similar lows as in the European polls.

Foreign Minister Erkki Tuomioja analysed the EU's crisis on his webpage after the June summit, saying that the problem was, to a large extent, due to the fact that people were turned off by the grand visions and rhetoric that the constitutional process engendered, even though the text itself might not be in any way offensive to them. Tuomioja, a leftist Social Democrat, said that the EU needs less high-flying rhetoric and results that are more practical, more work to create a social Europe, and a common foreign and security policy that is based on functioning multilateralism.

Sweden

The Swedish prime minister, Göran Persson, did not want the Swedes to vote on the constitutional treaty. He was afraid that it would be a 'no', but the Swedes, contrary to so many other countries, are not sceptical because they fear immigration or are afraid of losing influence, but more because they believe that the Swedish way is the best way and that they can manage on their own. Most of the Swedish political parties are divided on questions about the EU, and this has put a damper on the Swedish debate. The Social Democratic party, which has been in power for the last 40 years, is especially fearful that the division concerning EU questions will lead to a division within the party. Göran Persson was probably very relieved to be able to inform the press and the population that a Swedish referendum on the constitutional treaty had been shelved.

If You Don't Want To Hear The Answer, Don't Ask The Question

by Ylva Nilsson

Ylva Nilsson is a freelance journalist and writer, former EU correspondent in Brussels for Svenska Dagbladet and Dagens Industri (1988-2000).

Never ask a question if you don't want to hear the answer. Mr Göran Persson, the Swedish prime minister, has no wish to hear his voters' verdict on the European Constitution so he never had the intention of asking. For a long time, this decision did not constitute a political problem. Public debates in Sweden on European issues are few and far between. There is therefore nothing unusual about the fact that the new Constitution for Europe (until the French and the Dutch voted against it) was an issue that was not picked up by media or the public at large. Also to have the European Constitution ratified by the Swedish parliament only, without a referendum, was approved by the five bigger (and basically pro-European) parties in the parliament. True, two small parties, the Greens and the Left Party, that form the main EU opposition in Sweden were doing all they could to create a public outcry over the fact that the Swedish establishment did not want to hear the opinion of the people. Accusations of the kind from the Left and the

Greens are not unusual and, on its own, would constitute no major worry for the governing Social Democrats.

But, during spring 2005, other worries attached themselves to the list. Anti-EU activists within the Social Democratic party threatened to organise a members' vote within the party on the holding of a referendum. It would be most embarrassing for the leadership to lose such a vote. Also legal advice sought by the government turned out to be slightly ambiguous but leaning towards the necessity of changing the Swedish Constitution before ratifying the European Constitution – on account of the transfer of sovereignty – a cumbersome affair running over at least two parliaments.

Taken all together, the prime minister's stance on not holding a referendum started to become a political burden for the Social Democrats and at a very bad time from Mr Persson's point of view. General elections are coming up in September 2006. For a year now, his popularity ratings and those of his party have been at their lowest for many years.[14] As long as the debate stayed on the subject "Why Sweden would not hold a referendum", the problem was at least not a problem only for the Social Democrats.

Most of the Swedish MPs are against a referendum, the main argument being that the Constitution is such a complex collection of issues that it lends itself better to a parliamentary debate and decision. Presented to heated young people during a public debate, this argument, however, always did sound rather weak. "You're saying we're too stupid to have an opinion on the Constitution?" is the immediate retort. And the accusation follows: "You're afraid to ask in case we say no!"

Now, you could hardly blame Prime Minister Göran Persson and other pro-European politicians if the accusation was true and they were indeed afraid of a 'no' to the Constitution in a popular vote. The Swedish citizens are, after all, the biggest Euro-sceptics in the European Union, according to a number of Eurobarometer polls,[15] only occasionally beaten by the British or the Danish public. However, this scepticism bears little resemblance to the Euro-sceptic debate taking place in the rest of Europe.

---

[14] The SOM-Institute (Society, Opinion, Media) at the Gothenburg University announced in April 2005 that their latest polls revealed a very strong loss of personal popularity for Mr Göran Persson, even from among his own party members. Exact figures will be published in June 2005. As for his party, the Social Democrats, in April 2005 their support was down to 31.3% according to an opinion poll done by the polling institute Sifo, which is the lowest figure in eight years.

[15] Eurobarometer of December 2004 confirms this. In the EU as a whole (25 countries) only 13% considered the EU a bad thing, whereas 24% of the Swedish interviewees agreed with this statement, as did 22% of the British and 17% of the Austrians.

For example, the Turkish question is not an issue in Sweden. Swedish voters rather welcome a Turkish membership, just as the Swedes were very much in favour of the last wave of enlargement. There is no xenophobic debate in Sweden, no expressed public fear of immigrants swamping the country and no political party arguing that the foreigners must go. Having lived with a rather large net immigration for decades, the Swedish public opinion seems to have no immediate problem with open borders.

Then there is the sovereignty debate. The threat of losing sovereignty does not get the same knee-jerk reaction that it seems to do in neighbouring Denmark, for example.

True, Swedes tend to think that the EU meddles in things it could well stay out of and the idea of interfering bureaucrats is enough to turn some people off Europe. But then again, most Swedes perceive the Swedish state as overly prying into things that should not concern it. The idea of Sweden being overrun, made irrelevant, turned into a 'footnote' country in Europe does not really take hold in the Swedish mind, judging by the political debates and media coverage. There is no basic fear of losing the nation's independence. The word Union scares no one and hasn't caused a fuss like it did in other European countries. Rather, it brings back sentimental memories of a time when the Swedes used to bully the Norwegians (a union forced upon the Norwegians that fell apart in 1905). The truth is that Swedes perceive Sweden as a big country, a country with a lot of influence internationally. The explanation for this somewhat surprising perception can be found in Swedish history – a country that has never been conquered but has been the conqueror of German states, Russia and of Poland. In its Nordic part of Europe, Sweden has been a dominating country for centuries; Norway and Finland have both been Swedish colonies in the past.

All the same, the issue of sovereignty does explain why the Swedes are counted among the most Euro-sceptic people in the European Union, if you look at the question from an angle other than that of a nation's independence. This can be summarised as a feeling of "We're doing fine on our own; the Swedish way is a better way."[16] Here's why: The commonly

16 Olof Pettersson, professor in political sciences and head of research at Studieförbundet Näringsliv och Samhälle (the Centre for Business and Policy Studies or SNS), finds that this very attitude of "Sweden is superior and has nothing to learn from others" to be one of three main perceived ideas held by the Swedish people towards the EU membership. "The idea of Swedish superiority is deeply rooted, more than anything when it comes to welfare and democracy. The main reason to join the EU was (thus) to offer a sort of development aid. The other Europeans ought to be thankful to us for joining. It is with a mixture of surprise and irritation that Swedes realise that the others do not immediately and completely adopt the Swedish model. Even more surprising is the fact that we are asked to make changes when every change by definition must be for the worse." (Har svensk demokrati påverkats av EU-medlemskapet?, Tio år I EU, SNS, 2005.)

accepted myth and version of more recent European history is that Sweden managed to stay out of the war by being clever and sensible, by choosing the right way – neutrality. The myth and the Swedish version of European economic history is that Sweden has built its wealth on hard work and discipline. The version of how this society came to be so relatively peaceful and safe is that Swedes are good at cooperation and compromise.

The strong conviction that Sweden can go it alone was however badly shaken in the late 1980s and early 1990s. At the time, Sweden was undergoing its biggest economic crisis since the 1930s. Unemployment was at its highest level ever; cutbacks on schools, hospital care and social insurance were announced daily; some of the larger banks were threateningly close to bankruptcy. The suggestion from the Social Democratic party, in government in 1990, to apply for membership to the EU came as part of a whole package of measures to beat the economic crisis. Joining the EU was seen as the fast way to economic recovery.

The opposition to an EU membership came from the left wing.[17] Their underlying reasoning was that Sweden had nothing to gain but everything to lose – harmonising with Europe must surely mean going backwards, on all accounts. Sweden would be forced to dismantle its public sector, the very guarantee for equal distribution of welfare. Sweden would have to accept foreign, low-quality goods, and lower its environmental and public health standards. Swedes would have to lower their wages to European levels in order to compete. In short, the Swedish model, which stands for all good things, such as neutrality, equality of chances, generous welfare, secure and peaceful surroundings, fresh air and clean water, would be shot to pieces.

Dr Arthur Gould, senior lecturer in the Department of Social Sciences Studies, Loughborough University, discusses in several of his works the same Swedish attitude, particularly apparent when it comes to welfare issues. He notes how Swedes tend to feel, when faced with European influences, "under attack from alien forces". (Developments in this Swedish Social Policy: Resisting Dionysus, Palgrave, London, 2001.)

The Swedish attitude of knowing so much more than our fellow Europeans is revealed through a series of interviews with a large number of representatives from national authorities and courts, conducted by Kommerskollegium (National Board of Trade) in the course of reporting on how Sweden has taken on board the single market. The authors of the reports note that an overwhelming majority of civil servants declare Swedish laws to be generally of a much higher quality than EU legislation. More worrying, a number of civil servants feel that this 'fact' justifies dragging out or even avoiding implementation of EU legislation, and declare their conviction that this attitude is tolerated and acceptable to their superiors in the ministries. (Kommerskollegium, Rapporter om inre marknaden, May 2005.)

[17] According to the National Statistics Bureau (SCB), 80% of people voting for the Liberal or Conservative parties declare themselves positive to the EU, whereas only 45% of Social Democrats share that attitude, 30% of the Greens and less than 20% of the Left Party's voters. (EU-sympatier efter parti, SCB 2004.)

In the end, all these potential threats must have been less scary than the actual hard times people were living in. In the November 1994 referendum, 52.3% of the Swedish population said 'yes' to EU membership. According to research, it was the economic argument that won the day.[18] The stronghold of the no-campaign was found among women employed by the public sector, among people with lower education and salaries, as well as among those living in the sparsely populated extreme north. 'Yes' voters dominated amongst the younger, better-educated Swedes from urban areas.[19]

The ten years of EU membership that has followed do not seem to have changed the Swedish society irreparably, but the European debate, on the other hand, has. It created a highly uncomfortable situation that comes back to haunt the political establishment every time Europe is once more in the public eye. Behind the discomfort lies the fact that the dominating Social Democratic party (in power for more than 40 of the last 50 years) during the debate for or against EU membership was practically split down the middle between pro- and anti-EU. Fearing the party would fall apart, the leadership decided in 1994, even though the official line was pro-EU, that the party would not only allow but also finance outspoken opposition to the EU from its own members. In fact, as a gesture to heal the party after the referendum, several no-campaigners were offered seats in the government.

Over the years, other Swedish political parties have experienced the same problem of holding their party together on European issues. The Centre Liberal party has a split almost as big as the Social Democrats. The Conservatives and Christian Democrats both have a number of no-campaigners. The two anti-EU parties, the Greens and the Left Party, have pro-Europeans in their midst. This state of affairs makes the EU a sensitive topic among Swedish politicians and may well be one reason why the Swedish debate on Europe has been rather subdued over the years.

---

[18] The economy was ranked as the number one argument for voting 'yes' by 40% of the yes-voters with 'fear of isolation' mentioned as the second most important argument (30%) and 'peace' as number three (27%) in interviews done by The Institute of Electoral Research at the Gothenburg University. (Maria Oskarsson: Ett knappt ja till EU: väljarna och folkomröstningen, published in 1996, Norstedts juridik.)

[19] In the referendum of 1994, the highest percentage of yes-voters was found in Stockholm, Malmö, Gothenburg and other major cities, with the lowest percentage of yes-voters in the northern province of Jamtland and other northern provinces where the yes-voters barely made it over 20%. All in all, 58% of people living in rural areas voted 'no' with only 34% voting 'no' in urban areas; 41% of the workers voted 'yes' as opposed to 59% of white-collar workers; 48% of the women voted 'yes' in 1994 as opposed to 57% of the men. In 2004, 36% of the women declared themselves positive to the EU with 51.6% of the men. (SCB, Partisympatiundersökningar 1992-2004, Regionfakta and Maria Oskarsson and Sören Holmberg of the Institute of Electoral Research at the Gothenburg University as published in *EU – ett manligt medelklassprojekt?* and *Socioekonomisk gruppröstning.*)

The EU does not let itself be forgotten though. In 2002, the European countries had gone ahead according to plan and introduced the euro. The Swedish prime minister decided to take the plunge and ask the Swedish people about giving up the Swedish krona for the euro. The pro-Europe campaigners again tried the peace argument and then the economic argument. The no-campaigners got back, armed with economists that talked about risks and uncertainties with this European project and pointed at France's and Germany's failing economies and high unemployment. Their basic argument was that Sweden handles money matters better on its own, the Swedish way. When asked in September 2003 about giving up the Swedish krona in favour of the euro, the answer from 55.9% of the Swedish people was 'no'. Once again, the no-voters were mainly found among the category of underpaid women in the public sector, but this time also among the young.[20]

Losing the campaign was a bitter blow for Mr Persson personally. It did not make things easier that it was his own party members who helped bring him down. When the election to the European Parliament was held less than a year later, the pro-European parties seemed not to want to be bothered with more European debate. In the end, only a third of the Swedish voters turned up and they gave an unheard-of 15% to a most unlikely new party, led by elderly men from the establishment (economists and industrialists), anti-EU but not very clear on how or why, except for it being overly bureaucratic. The Social Democrats had their worst election ever.

What are the chances that a debate and the outcome of a popular vote on the European Constitution would turn out more positive for the governing Social Democrats?

One needs to go to seminars at universities or look for specialised websites on the Internet to find any on-going debate on the European Constitution in Sweden. Here, the yes- and the no-sides are easily recognisable from earlier referendum campaigns.

The main argument in favour seems to be that the Constitution will give us a more open and democratic Union. LO, the national blue-collar union, argues that it gives unions a more solid standing and promotes the goal of 'full employment'. A common theme from the pro-Europeans is also that the Constitution really doesn't alter things very much.

---

[20] Sixty percent of the women voted 'no' and 38% 'yes', whereas among men it was 50-50; 62.3% of the young (18-20 years old) voted 'no'; 54.7% in Stockholm voted 'yes' but only 21.4% in the northern county of Jamtland; 57% of people with a university education voted 'yes' whereas 65.8% of people with no higher education voted 'no'. (SCB, National Statistics Office, Democracy Statistics, 2004.)

The no-side brings back the welfare argument, saying that the Constitution establishes market liberalism as a must for all member countries, thus forcing Sweden to do away with its large public sector. It is also argued that the Constitution obliges every member country to spend more on defence, using money that should go to schools, the elderly, and the poor. All in all, it looks safe to bet on yet another 'no' from the Swedes.

You may think that a refusal of the Constitution should not overly concern Mr Persson. After all, his line on all of the issues when the Constitution was negotiated – a president for Europe or not, voting rights for smaller countries, a commissioner from each country or not – were one and the same: Sweden can live with either alternative. But losing a referendum at this point could be the final straw that ousts the Social Democrats from power, given their weak domestic situation. A referendum would once again open that dangerous rift within the party. This could be costly with the general election a year from now, especially since a coalition of Liberal and Conservative parties have held a comfortable lead in the opinion polls for six months.[21]

Mr Persson is already running a minority government. And now there are new rivals appearing on the political scene. A number of well-known women are setting up a political party called the Feminist Initiative and intend to run in the next elections.

Feminist issues are high on the Swedish political agenda and 11% of the voters so far say they may vote for FI, according to market analyst Demoskop. Also, the anti-EU coalition, Junilistan, seems intent on running in the election and could possibly win over some of the many anti-EU Social Democrats.

At the EU summit in June 2005, Mr Persson did not wait for the decision to postpone the ratification of the European Constitution before he announced to the Swedish press that the Swedish ratification was off the agenda. And with the high Swedish fee for EU membership and the heavy subsidising of farmers being favourite hate objects in any anti-EU campaign, Mr Persson happily took the plunge alongside the British prime minister in refusing a budget deal at the summit. Being unpopular among the European leaders or deepening a crisis of the EU are not Mr Persson´s major worries. A non-ratification couldn't possibly have been more welcome.

---

[21] According to the Swedish polling institute, Sifo, in June 2005 the Conservative-Liberal alliance had 52.1% of the voter's, while the Social Democrats with their two supporting parties, the Left and the Greens, stood at 44.2 %.

Austria

Fear of isolation was the main reason Austria wanted to be admitted into the European Union and fear has marked the country's relationship with the EU ever since. In the beginning, it was fear concerning the introduction of the euro, then fear of the enlargement and, lastly, it was fear that their small country would drown in the political game with the larger Member States. It is, thus, not surprising that the Austrian government didn't want to increase the insecurity by initiating a large debate about the constitutional treaty. The treaty was therefore ratified in the parliament, without too many problems, in spite of the fact that Austria is among the most EU-sceptical nation in the partnership. The French 'no' finally kick-started the debate in Austria and the sceptical attitudes started to take form.

Fear Sets The Agenda

by Wolfgang Böhm (translated by Tom Feeley)

Wolfgang Böhm is a journalist and head of the European section of the daily newspaper, Die Presse, in Vienna.

In analysing the attitudes of Austrians towards the EU, there is one word that crops up again and again which sums up their feelings: fear. The country joined the EU in 1995 because of a fear of being left on its own. Isolation threatened Austria, both economically and politically, in a Europe that was becoming more and more integrated. "Together instead of alone" was the slogan of the then government's campaign to support EU accession and it summed up the opinion of the population perfectly.

Since joining the EU, fear has also dominated their membership. In the beginning there was the fear surrounding the introduction of the euro, then the fear of enlargement, and finally the fear that, as a small country, she would not be able to assert herself against the larger Member States.

This anxiety became a kind of self-fulfilling prophecy as the feelings of helplessness and the fear of being marginalised as a small state led to continuous tensions between Austria and its EU partners. The government increased these tensions by becoming an often-unpredictable negotiating partner, blocking the enlargement process on more than one occasion. The problems came to a head in the year 2000 with the EU's diplomatic measures (sanctions) taken against the Austrian government coalition partner, the populist right wing Freedom Party (Freiheitliche Partei Österreichs or FPÖ). At the time, the 14 other EU Member States decided to ostracise the irksome Austrian government partner and, in doing so, confirmed the fears of a large section of the population towards the EU. This had fatal consequences on the attitudes of the majority of Austrians towards the EU.

Today, it is mainly the less well-educated and elderly Austrians who are more sceptical about EU membership than ever before, says the Austrian Society for European Policy survey (ÖGfE, April 2005). While the FPÖ have become the focal point for Euro-scepticism in recent years, the once EU-critical Greens have changed into a pro-Europe party. Of the voters of the Christian democratic Austrian People's Party (ÖVP) and the Greens, 86% see no reason to leave the EU at this time with 70% of the Social Democratic Party (SPÖ) sharing this view. According to the ÖGfE survey, exactly half of FPÖ supporters were in favour of leaving the EU.

Leaving the Union is not really regarded as an option by the Austrian people. It is more the fear of future effects of EU membership than a concrete wish to leave the Union that has sparked the Austrian scepticism. At present, the Austrians express concerns about losing their jobs to their neighbouring countries that have recently joined the EU. According to a Eurobarometer survey (No. 62, autumn 2004), they also fear an increase in drug dealing and petty crime as a result of the opening up of borders to central and eastern European countries. In addition, they fear losing more influence in Europe whilst at the same time having to pay more into the EU coffers in Brussels.

It is not really surprising that the Austrian federal government wants to avoid generating a new uncertainty amongst the population by promoting widespread public debate about the EU Constitution. The EU Constitution, currently the most important issue surrounding European integration, is avoided by most parties in Austrian national politics like ships avoiding a large iceberg.

Federal Chancellor Wolfgang Schüssel of the ÖVP party succeeded in getting a political green light for the Constitution due to the suppressed public debate and the positive support the text received from most parties in parliament. The only critical opinions towards the Constitution and demands for a national referendum came from Schüssel's coalition partner, the Freedom Party (part of which has become the BZÖ or Bündnis Zukunft Österreich) and Hans-Peter Martin who ran in the European elections with his own list. The Greens also argued from time to time in favour of a referendum but were never very emphatic about it.

Eventually the Federal chancellor managed to bring round the Freedom Party ministers who had, up until then, been more critical of the EU and, in doing so, he cleared the way for the European Constitution in the government. It was an almost silent ratification in Austria when, on 30 March 2005, the constitutional treaty was adopted by the Council of Ministers and sent on to the parliament. On 11 May, the treaty was debated in the National Assembly and then adopted with a large majority. Only one member of parliament, Mrs. Barbara Rosenkranz from the Freedom Party, voted against the Constitution.

The SPÖ opposition party also contributed to the unproblematic ratification, having spoken out in clear favour of the European Constitution from the start. As the largest opposition party, they would also not have insisted on a referendum. The SPÖ's European spokesman, Caspar Einem, argued in July 2004 at a press briefing in Vienna that a referendum was not necessary because the EU Constitution did not lead to any complete changes of the Federal Constitution. Einem said, "The adoption of the new Constitution for Europe is to be welcomed" and that the Constitution would be "better than the one that was used up to now".

The ÖVP, led by Schüssel, supported the EU Constitution without any reservations. The Greens were also for the new EU Constitution in spite of some critical voices from the more extreme left-wing part of the party. One reason for the support of the Greens was the fact that the prominent Green MEP, Johannes Voggenhuber, was part of the constitutional convention. Additionally, he defended the Constitution against attacks levelled at the text by left-wing groups.

The criticism towards the European Constitution was concentrated within the far right, nationalistic factions of the FPÖ, who along with left-orientated, extra-parliamentary groups like the communists (KPÖ) and the anti-globalisation group, Attac, had been against advances in European integration for many years. As in Germany, Attac also warned in Austria of the establishment of fundamental neo-liberal values via the European Constitution. According to the organisation, the social-market economy will be infiltrated by strengthened competition. The more extreme, left-wing sections of the Greens were in close contact with Attac so the Green MEP, Johannes Voggenhuber, stepped in to prevent them adopting their arguments. In newspaper interviews and public discussions, he tried to convince people that supporters of neo-liberalism on the constitutional convention had suffered a defeat. According to the prominent Green, any wording in the third part of the text that could be read as neo-liberal was brought into the treaty by the European Council. He claims the Convention on the future of Europe should not be blamed but, instead, the current balances of political power in Europe.

The relatively unproblematic ratification of the constitutional treaty should not draw away from the fact that Austria is still amongst the most Euro-sceptical of Member States. In the past, Austria had already proved itself to be negative, stalling public debate on important questions of European integration. It was because of this that the presence of the Euro-sceptic FPÖ led the government to hold back on a widespread information campaign on EU enlargement. To a large extent, Austrians were therefore unprepared for the accession of their neighbouring countries to the East.

The inadequate public debate on enlargement also led to fears and anxieties being heightened instead of being overcome. According to a Eurobarometer survey (No. 62, autumn 2004), 76% of Austrians are worried about a transfer of jobs to new EU Member States. Actually the only people who rationally could have worries are those living in the border regions. By and large, Austria has already profited greatly from the opening up of the East following the fall of the iron curtain. According to the Viennese Institute for International Economic Comparison (WIIW, May 2005), the gradual opening up of the markets in neighbouring ex-communist countries after 1989 brought about 6% extra economic growth (around 14,000 million euro) and around 60,000 extra jobs in the first ten years. WIIW has also predicted a positive impetus on Austria caused by the relatively high growth in the new EU Member States. It has shown that instead of there being a shift of production to neighbouring countries, Austrian firms have in fact profited greatly from new business with the East.

The topic of Turkey also showed how restricted public debate could have an adverse effect. In December 2004, the decision by the European Council to start accession talks with the Turkish government was again met by unprepared Austrians. Federal Chancellor Wolfgang Schüssel had until then restricted domestic political debate about the continuing political process. In spite of their critical positions, the SPÖ and the Greens did not want to touch the delicate topic so as not to stir up anti-foreigner sentiments. The Freedom Party stepped in against the accession of Turkey but, due to internal party problems, did not have the power to get their position across in the government. The negative emotions of the population really exploded as the decision of the European Council to start accession talks with Turkey was made public at the end of 2004. According to surveys in the meantime, 73% of Austrians are against Turkey's EU membership (Survey of Sozialwissenschaftlichen Studiengesellschaft SWS, December 2004). In order to cool down the heated debate that had sprung out of nowhere, Chancellor Schüssel talked of holding a referendum in Austria concerning

Turkey's accession. The referendum would take place once the accession negotiations with Ankara had finished.

A similar information vacuum that appeared during the enlargement and Turkey's EU membership is now showing itself with the EU Constitution. The government made free copies of the Constitution text available for all interested citizens and had brochures printed summarising all the important points. However, a broad explanation of the text to citizens has yet again not taken place. On top of this, the Austrian broadcasting corporation (ÖRF) has not provided information, apart from a few exceptions, and the same goes for most of the country's printed media. The media hardly covered the development of the Constitution debate in countries like France because, domestically, it had not really been discussed and was not controversial or exciting enough.

Whilst the SPÖ and the Greens denounced the suppressed debate as the fault of the government, representatives of the governing ÖVP claimed to be extremely satisfied with the situation. MEP Ursula Stenzel defended the position of her party's leader, Wolfgang Schüssel, by saying, "I don't think we need to make much ado about nothing." The Constitution would not really be disputed in Austria anyway.

As with the Turkey debate, the debate on the Constitution also showed that the withholding of important European issues has a counter-productive effect. Following the French 'non' to the EU Constitution and the Dutch 'nee' a few days later, the debate suddenly exploded in Austria. Whilst beforehand the population had still been able to see many positive aspects of the Constitution, they now saw them as negative. According to a published Gallup survey in spring 2005, around two thirds (67%) of Austrians were in favour of the Constitution and only 15% against (the rest were undecided). The mood in Austria really reached its low point after the French referendum. As a consequence of the no-vote, many Austrians also found it in themselves to publicly voice their concerns about the EU and a way round the Constitution. According to an OGM survey from 30 May 2005, the proportion of people against the Constitution reached 43% compared with the 29% who were still in favour. Also 28% were unsure how they would vote if a popular referendum were to be held in Austria.

The problem is certainly not the consent of the people but a lack of knowledge. According to a Eurobarometer survey (Special 214, Nov. 2004), 28% of Austrians had not even heard of the Constitution before the autumn of 2004, 61% knew of its existence but knew little about its content and a mere 11% felt fully informed. It was indicative that Austria's chancellor, Wolfgang Schüssel, suddenly started a final rescue attempt following the June 2005 EU summit where the EU's heads of government decided on having a 'period of reflection' for the Constitution. Although the Constitution had already been declared dead in many countries, just three days after the summit, Schüssel announced a widespread discussion on the legal text that had become so disputed. "Both the parliament and social partners as well as the public shall be involved in the dialogue." Perhaps a little self-criticism by the chancellor also played a role in this decision.

It not surprising that Austrians were not entirely interested in this treaty. From the beginning, the federal government has not really attached a great meaning to the Constitution process and in public speeches has played down its importance. The former finance minister, Hannes Farnleitner, was chosen by Chancellor Schüssel to represent the government at the constitutional convention. Farnleitner is known to be a close ally of the chancellor's but he is not known as a constitutional expert or as a political heavyweight. What the ex-minister did however work on was building coalitions in the Convention with smaller EU states. As part of the European Council, Wolfgang Schüssel himself also sought to draw together a group of smaller countries including Sweden, Austria, Ireland, Luxembourg, Finland and Portugal. Schüssel's goals relating to the content of the Constitution were to keep the principle whereby each Member State has their own commissioner with their own vote and to prevent larger Member States acting as a board of directors. Schüssel said, "During the negotiations I always found the group of like-minded states as a positive element. Due to their dedicated cooperation, the negotiations could be closed quickly. The agreed text guarantees that Europe will not become a superstate and the basic rights of the members will remain. National parliaments will also have greater inclusion in the future."

In spite of Schüssel's positive résumé, the group of smaller EU states' actions did not translate to any great success, either at the Convention or at the final council summit. Neither the efforts to keep a commissioner with voting rights nor the efforts against an elected council President seemed to bring results. Little by little, the front line of the 'smalls' seemed to be broken down. Austria was not able to get its way on the points that it had earlier defined as being important. According to the Constitution, after the current transition period, the Brussels-based EU commission will be reduced to 15 commissioners. The elected Council President that many smaller states wanted to avoid is also fixed in the text. In addition, Austria's reservations against stronger cooperation of the judiciary did not win a majority.

At the same time, there were certainly some smaller successes. Actions over water resources will continue to be decided by unanimity, which is emotively very important in Austria. It means it is not possible for any EU state to out-vote another. This decision quashed fears that via qualified majority voting (QMV), other EU partners could get hold of Austria's water resources or a Europe-wide commercialisation of them would be possible against the will of the country.

The strengthening of military cooperation would have also been of domestic relevance as the European Constitution plans it. The political parties of Austria also restricted widespread public dialogue even here. The government dismissed concerns by individual constitutional experts that the EU Constitution could further weaken Austria's neutrality. In this case the federal government played cleverly with time, as the Constitution only brings up further cooperation under defence questions, Austria will not have to make a decision about this until a later date. This was greeted with criticism from the Greens and the SP... but they did not see increased military cooperation as a negative aspect. They were traditionally against a connection of their country with the Atlantic union. In their opinion, greater military cooperation in Europe reduces the meaning of the North Atlantic Pact (NATO). "I'm happy about this," said the Green MEP, Johannes Voggenhuber; had the EU already decided on the future of its security policy "it would have been in favour of NATO".

The former Austrian EU Commissioner, Franz Fischler, pointed out though that the country cannot put off the debate about the future of neutrality forever. "Austria will not come around to this decision," he said in an interview with the daily newspaper, Die Presse.

As with the question of security policy, the lack of debate on the European Constitution shows that ten years after its accession, Austria is still not quite settled in the EU. Groundbreaking decisions at the European level will not be taken as such. The decision-making processes will not be accompanied by a public debate. Instead of the opportunity as a small country to jointly develop and form via public debate, the government with its passive discussion culture has in fact strengthened the population's feeling of helplessness towards its predecessors in the European Union.

Poland

The fall of the Berlin wall created a feeling among the Poles of the EU being a guarantor for peace, security and progress. Membership was a crowning achievement after ten years of hard reforms in order to comply with the membership criteria, and Poland is still one of the most EU-positive countries in Europe. To the Poles, the EU symbolises security, even though they are aware that the full advantages of their membership will not be felt until the next generation. Still, even in Poland, certain scepticism can be found. The criticism concerns the distribution of voting weights and the missing reference to Christianity in the constitutional treaty.

Still A Happy Newcomer

by Krzysztof Bobiński

Krzysztof Bobiński is currently at the Unia & Polska Foundation, a pro European Polish NGO. He was the Financial Times correspondent in Warsaw from the mid seventies until 2000 and he published Unia & Polska, a magazine devoted to European affairs from 1998 to 2003.

A jinx seems to hang over Poland. At the end of the 18th century, the country was partitioned by Russia, Austria, and Prussia and caught in a grip, which successive armed uprisings failed to loosen. The independence, which came at the end of the Great War in 1918, lasted for just over two decades, and then the onset of the Second World War saw occupation by both the Soviets and the German Nazis. In 1945, the end of the war saw the Soviet Union establish its dominance over Poland and the other Central and Eastern European states.

The last two hundred years have seen the country unable to develop either politically or economically as a sovereign state as its educated elites were depleted as a result of armed conflict, deportation and emigration. It was only in 1989 that Poles felt that they were safe. When the Berlin Wall fell, membership in two seemingly very stable organisations, NATO and the European Union, became a reality. Instinctively, Poles, like other societies that have gone through traumatic events, felt their destiny was with these two organisations that stood for security, peace and prosperity. But the jinx still seems to be there. For even as Poland joined NATO, that alliance immediately went to war against Serbia for the first time in its history. Now, a year after joining the European Union, the Brussels-based organisation faces a major crisis of confidence with the constitutional treaty in trouble and the prospect of major rifts if it fails to come into force.

How much of these developments can be ascribed to the Poles themselves and how much is beyond their control is a moot point. Certainly, the very nature of NATO, and probably less so of the European Union, has changed because of the fact that the former Soviet bloc countries have joined. Also much of the present unhappiness with the European Union is caused by fears that enlargement, coming at a time of economic downturn, will further depress living standards in the 'old' Member States. But with the majority of Poles happy with the fact that their country is now an EU member, it has been left to the political and intellectual elites to conduct a punishing debate on the EU. However, this debate doesn't affect the Polish membership, though it could undermine the benefits that Poland stands to reap if its commitment to the EU was wholehearted.

In countries like France, much of the populace seems to be unhappy about the direction in which the EU is going and it is the better educated who show more enthusiasm for the European project. In contrast, support in Poland for the EU remains high. Poland joined the European Union along with nine other candidates (eight of them from the former Soviet Bloc) on 1 May 2004. That moment was preceded by a decade of preparations, which saw the European Commission in Brussels dictating painful conditions of membership. Economic adjustments affected major industries such as coal and steel. The accession negotiations were seen as being unfair to farmers who couldn't believe that they would be beneficiaries of the Common Agricultural Policy. Nevertheless, when the accession referendum was held in June 2003, 77.45% of those voting said 'yes' on a turnout of 58.85%. This result was in line with polling on the EU during the accession negotiations that saw support stay stable at around 70%.[22] Indeed, after the first year of membership, polls in April 2005 showed support actually rising to 79%.[23]

Support remained high after accession even though politicians had assumed that post-accession price rises and the general feeling of being bullied and short-changed by the European Union would bring a wave of anti-Brussels

---

[22] For referendum results see State Electoral Commission website: www.pkw.gov.pl. For attitudes to the European Union see results from the Centrum Badan Opinii Publicznej (CBOS).
[23] CBOS April 2005, BS/79/2005.

sentiment. Thus, they began to position themselves to take advantage of a worsening of sentiment. Indeed the dispute between Poland and Spain and the other Member States during the IGC on the constitutional treaty over the voting weights in the European Council and the lack of a clear reference to Christianity in the preamble to the treaty seemed like a good opportunity to stake out Euro-sceptic positions. But even though between the accession referendum in the summer of 2003 and Polish acceptance of a compromise on the treaty the argument was loud and furious, support for the EU only dipped by around ten percentage points for several months, and after the accession in May 2004 rose to higher than before.[24]

What the politicians, especially those on the right wing of the spectrum, had failed to factor in was that the European Union symbolises long-term security for the mass of the population who know they do not want to be left outside the EU. For this reason, people want to be in the European Union even though they understand the relative under-development of their economy and the gulf in prosperity between the old member state economies and their own. As people declare their support for the EU, they admit that membership would favour their children but know that the country is unprepared.[25] Many agreed with the politicians that the first years might be difficult but that they were willing to put up with it for the greater prizes, which were long-term security and the prospect of a modern and prosperous state.

Up until the accession referendum, the mainstream political parties maintained a consensus on support for membership. The only parties that were opposed were the right-wing, ultra catholic League of Polish Families (LPR or Liga Polskich Rodzin) and the populist Self Defence (Samobrona) movement. The former party remains at the core of anti-EU sentiment. It argues against the fact of a transfer of sovereignty to the Union and maintains that the EU is dominated by Germany and France, with the former portrayed as Poland's historical enemy with whom rapprochement is

---

[24] CBOS, July 2004 BS/115/2004.

[25] In one study in 2000, Poles were asked to pick the animal which best identified them in their dealings with the EU. They chose a mouse. Most identified the tiger with the European Commission. (Janusz Grelak, Dominika Maison, Grazyna Wąsowicz-Kiryło, Kultura negocjacyjna Polaków w kontekście integracji z UE, ISP Warszaw 2000.) Also CBOS surveys showed that Poles felt that the country was unprepared for membership and that the 'old' Member States would gain more from enlargement. In a CBOS poll carried out at the beginning of February 2003 (CBOS, February 2003, BS/39/2003), 47% thought this would be the case while 26% thought that both sides would gain and a mere 9% would see Poland gain at the expense of the old Member States. The same poll showed that 47% thought that the Polish economy was unprepared, while a further 38% thought that Poland should join as soon as possible in order to modernise the economy. Yet these doubts did not stop almost two-thirds of Poles participating in the accession referendum five months later with over three-quarters of those voting 'yes'.

impossible. The LPR is backed by the traditionalist wing of the Catholic Church and a catholic radio station called Radio Maryja, which is widely listened to by the LPR's electorate. It is Radio Maryja that articulates the view that the European Union is an organisation which is programmed to destroy the Polish nation by imposing liberal values, be they in the field of sexual behaviour, social norms or in the economic field where untrammelled competition from foreign firms will destroy Polish-owned firms.

The views of Samobrona, a populist party that seeks support by generating an atmosphere of generalised protest, are less well defined. After all, in the last European Parliament it fielded a team of candidates well qualified to deal with issues at the European Parliament level but who campaigned on the following slogan – the party that is able to say 'no' – without defining what it would say 'no' to. At the other end of the spectrum was the left of centre, post-communist Left Democratic Alliance (SLD or Sojusz Lewicy Demokratycznej), which took Poland into the EU. The SLD never hesitated to argue that membership was an opportunity to develop and modernise the country and anchor it firmly in the west. A similar position was adopted by the Freedom Union (UW or Unia Wolności), which lost its place in parliament in the 2001 election. The right-wing Law and Justice (PiS or Prawo i Sprawiedliwość), which is currently well placed to play a leading role in the administration that will be elected in the September 2005 election always took a more Euro-sceptic line. Membership of the European Union was a necessity for Poland, they admitted, but the EU that the PiS wanted to see was a 'Europe of nations'. Indeed this was the group that PiS joined when it entered the European Parliament in June 2004. For PiS, the European Union was an unwanted necessity and it took every opportunity to signal to its supporters that it treated the EU with the greatest mistrust.

More confusing still, was the line taken by the Civic Platform (PO or Platforma Obywatelska) whose leaders, such as Jan Rokita, declared that they were federalists but chose to oppose the constitutional treaty, tooth and nail. The Civic Platform is in theory pro-European but in practice, whether on the Constitution or budget issues, opposes the European consensus and argues that Poland could gain more advantage for itself by saying 'no' and holding out for better terms.

Despite its pro-EU stance, the left-leaning SLD government decided at the intergovernmental conference (IGC) to oppose the change in voting weights, which the draft constitutional treaty proposed. Poland, like Spain, lost the 27 votes that it had been awarded at Nice (compared to the 29 allocated to Germany, France, Italy and the United Kingdom). Instead, the weight of votes was to reflect the size of the populations of the countries and Polish strategists saw that this would make it more difficult to block decisions unfavourable to the new Member States. Knowing that Spain was also opposed to the change, Leszek Miller chose to defy France and Germany on the issue. He explained that following his experiences at the Copenhagen summit in December 2003 when he had hammered out a deal which he was able to sell to the Poles as favourable, he thought this was the way to produce results. "In Copenhagen we won out by adopting a tough stance. I have seen Member States demanding things and getting them. Why should Poland have behaved any differently? Why should we say 'yes' when we could get more by refusing to say 'yes'," Miller said later.[26] The right-wing opposition, which felt anything but positive about Miller's administration, gritted its teeth and decided to back him to the hilt. Jan Rokita, from the Civic Platform, the pro-business party, said that for him the issue was 'Nice or death' and that slogan became the catchword for the Polish campaign in the IGC.

Leszek Miller, whose administration had been steadily losing popular support, resigned as Poland joined the EU. He was succeeded by a caretaker cabinet headed by Marek Belka, who did a deal on the Constitution at the EU summit in June 2004. In any case, the Polish position had become untenable after the Socialist government in Spain decided to drop its support for Nice. The decision was greeted with dismay by the right-wing opposition, which had steadfastly supported the post-communists in their defence of the Nice formula. After the signing of the treaty in Rome in October 2004, they quickly realised that there was a chance that other Member States, like the United Kingdom, might not ratify the constitutional treaty. The French and Dutch results surpassed their wildest dreams. All that they had to do was to wait for more countries to decapitate the treaty for them. After France and Holland, they declared that the treaty was dead and their main aim remains to hold the Polish referendum as late as possible.

During the discussions in the IGC, Poland and Spain held out against the rest of the EU. The main arguments in Poland in defence of the government stance was that the Nice formulas had given Poland a strong position in the EU and that now this was being taken away. Secondly, the Poles were unhappy that the Christian tradition of the continent had not been adequately underlined in the preamble to the treaty.

The prospect that other countries might vote down the treaty took the fire out of the Polish debate. At the same time, it became increasingly clear to supporters of the treaty that the Polish referendum should take place as soon as possible, preferably together with the presidential elections in October 2005 as this provided the best chance of boosting the turnout to over the 50% mark required by the Polish Constitution to make the vote valid.

---

[26]See Miller interview quoted in Krzysztof Bobiński, Po referendum – nowa jakość polskiej debaty europejskiej? in 'Obywatele Europy' Instytut Spraw Publicznych, Warsaw 2005.

However, when the Brussels Summit in June 2005 agreed to allow more time for reflection, and countries like Denmark and Ireland decided to delay, then the treaty supporters lost heart. Simply it became unfeasible to persuade people to turn out and vote when the process had been postponed elsewhere. Accordingly, President Aleksander Kwasniewski looked to parliament to vote for a referendum but admitted that the plebiscite would take place no earlier than 2006. So in effect, the argument in Poland was procedural and not substantive.

During the IGC, the arguments for and against the Polish position were high on the media agenda. Parliament held as many as six plenary debates on the subject in the space of a year. Once the deal was done by Prime Minister Belka, the subject of Europe disappeared from the media and popular apathy engulfed the issue of the new EU treaty. Should the Polish referendum be held then the arguments over the bad deal Poland got when it was forced to drop the Nice formula would resurface. So would the question of Christianity in the preamble. The right will no doubt return to its theme that the treaty marks the beginning of a German-French condominium in Europe, although that maybe made less credible after the French no-vote.

The no-campaign will be supported by the right-wing Prawo i Sprawiedliwość (PiS) (Law and Justice) party, which is sure to be part of the next government administration elected in 2005 in parliamentary elections. The PiS coalition partner in government will most probably be the Civic Platform (PO), which is still officially opposed to the treaty. This is despite the fact that large swathes of the party are more favourably disposed, especially as they can see the opinion polls, which say that three-quarters of those who can be bothered to vote in the referendum will vote for the treaty.[27]

The left-wing parties, which currently make up the government, will be hard put to get back into parliament at the next election, not because of their stance on Europe but because of the aura of corruption that has engulfed the outgoing administration. The other opposition party, the Partia Demokratyczna (PD, Partia Demokratyczna) and the successor party to the Unia Wolności, is uncompromisingly for the treaty but is too small to make much of an impact. The main concern of the pro-European NGOs, which will also campaign for a yes-vote, will be to get people out to vote. The main argument in the yes-campaign will have to be that a vote for the treaty will be a vote of confidence in the future of the European Union. The arguments against will be split. The PiS and the PO will take the line that they are for Europe but against the treaty as it weakens Poland's position in

---

[27] See the www.eureferenda.org website for the results of Polish polls after the French and Dutch referenda.

the EU. The uncompromising anti-EU parties like the League of Polish Families will campaign against on the grounds that Poland should never have entered the EU in the first place.

Were the Polish referendum to be held then it will most probably be won by the yes-camp because the majority of the population is still for EU membership. At the same time, the election will be won by PiS and PO, two parties whose leaderships have for the past two years made a habit of criticising the European Union with varying degrees of intensity. Support for the EU is one thing but the political leadership of Member States have to signal to their government administrations that they are content to work within the EU for the national and the common interest. Countries have to work with and not against their partners in the EU, or at least appear to be doing so if Member States are to count in the EU. That spirit will be lacking in the next government administration and that could well hurt Poland's position in the European Union.

The Czech Republic

The Czechs saw the accession to the EU as a one-way ticket away from communist dictatorship. The experiences from the Soviet rule have given the Czechs a savage resistance to being controlled by bigger powers, and this resistance is reflected in a strong criticism of France and Germany's domineering role in the EU partnership. The Czechs are also critical of the economic value of the partnership, for the great expectations of an even flow of financial aid have not been fulfilled. Since the accession, the interest in the EU has lessened and not even the politicians have a great deal of knowledge on the subject. The politicians blame the EU for all unpopular initiatives, but in spite of this, as well as in spite of a president who is directly against the treaty, the Czechs have no regrets about their membership. Opinion polls indicate that 63% of the Czech voters would have voted 'yes' to the constitutional treaty if they had been given the opportunity.

A One-Way Ticket To The West: The Czech Marriage Of Convenience To The EU

by Johanna Grohová

Johanna Grohová is a Brussels-based correspondent working for the Czech Mlada fronta DNES.

The Czechs, who once dreamed of becoming a member of the European Union, are now considered a very serious threat to the European Constitution; a bigger threat than any other new Member State, and maybe even more of a threat than the traditionally Euro-sceptic British. Regardless of having only recently joined, the European Union now represents an object of fear, boredom and lack of interest to many Czechs, rather than the dreamland. European affairs have gradually become a distant issue to most people and the European Union is much too complicated; people, including most politicians, do not follow its development. This is just part of the reason that has brought such a shift in the mood.

So, what makes Czechs so increasingly suspicious about the EU? Let's start with the national character. Czechs can get inspired by things and will fight for freedom as they did fifteen years ago, when they went out onto the streets and demanded the end of old communist structures and the start of longed-for democracy. The feeling of a newly acquired space and freedom brought back some national pride. The country was in the world's spotlight and the people, who were finally able to travel to the West, could get a glimpse of capitalistic democracy. Naturally, they started hoping to become as rich as the people living in the European Union. Everything seemed so easy and close by at that time. The future was bright.

It was the EU membership that represented the generally desired ticket, taking people away from the era of a communist regime, oppressed personal freedom, and a centrally planned economy. And the same ticket should have brought them back to the family of democratic and rich countries. EU membership and the joining of NATO were the main political targets for the near future.

It is now nearly a year since the Czech Republic and the other nine, mostly Central and Eastern European, post-communist countries joined 'the club', but the prosperity, seemingly so close, is still far away. For example, the Czechs will have to wait another forty years to reach the average income level of the citizens of Germany. However, the feeling of change connected with entry is absent, mainly because the new Member States have gone through years of preparation before they were able to meet all the criteria demanded by Brussels for membership. It required the screening of legislation to make it compliant with European law. Many new directives, which were often very demanding in terms of money and investment, had to be put in place. On the other hand, a lot of European money has come into the country through various pre-accession funds to build new roads and improve the environment, though the entire process took much longer than was originally expected; politicians talked about the end of the millennium, but the country had to wait a further five years.

However, it would be unfair and wrong to say that the majority of Czech citizens are now against the European integration or regret joining the structure. Regardless of the many alarming expectations that people had before the actual entry, none have really become everyday reality. People feared a rise in the price of food and housing, many Czech businesses and farmers feared they would have to declare bankruptcy because of a harsh competition from the West. Nothing like that has happened, certainly not to any great extent. Even the profound Euro-sceptical Czech president, Václav Klaus, admitted during his traditional New Year's speech, that the year 2004 hadn't brought many exceptional changes. What he meant was that the historic entry of the ten new members was mainly a symbolic act, because they had already been highly integrated during the previous few years. Ironically enough, just before the entry, Mr Klaus was stressing on nearly every suitable occasion that the Czech Republic would lose a great part of its sovereignty, which the people would very much regret later.

However, the EU is not an idol anymore. Now people dare to ask themselves: Do we really need to be in? Most of the countries will not let us work there anyway. We do not need the others to tell us what to do. This was something unthinkable a couple of years ago. The Union itself is partially responsible: it produces so many guidelines and directives but is not very good at explaining why. Czechs were, for example, astonished to discover that their goulash has to be thrown away after a couple of hours to meet all the strict hygiene conditions. And every Czech will tell you that this popular dish is best eaten at least one day after cooking. The Union also doesn't serve as the easy cash machine the people had originally expected from what their politicians kept telling them. The government somehow forgot to mention that cities and villages have to be able to submit quality projects in return for funding.

It is not only the question of new rules imposed on the Czechs that are sometimes hard to follow. The membership has also allowed people of the Czech Republic, a relatively small country, to see that it is the big countries that mainly rule the EU. The March EU summit, which eased the rules of the Stability Pact and postponed the liberalisation of the services, works as a recent example. It was France, backed by Germany, who pushed through these changes regardless of very different views, especially from new member countries but also some older ones, including Austria and the Netherlands. If you take all these mixed feelings and listen to the critics of the Constitution who claim that the document will give the big ones even more power, it is hard to persuade people of the opposite situation. And Czechs, as Mr Klaus would stress, are very sensitive to any big country imposing its will on them. For three hundred years, the Czechs lived within the Habsburg Empire and at one point their language was on the edge of extinction. Finally, in 1918, they acquired their independent state together with the Slovaks, but after only 20 years, it was smashed by Nazi Germany. Shortly after the Second World War, it was the Soviet Union that took charge for a further forty years until the communist block collapsed.

The local politicians can be called to account too, if we talk about the fading popularity of the European Union. It has become almost a national sport for many of them to use the Union as an excuse for anything unpopular that has to be approved. The government often argued: we are not responsible for this, it is required by Brussels and we just have to approve it for the sake of smooth membership. Many times it was a crystal-clear lie, as when the Ministry of Health ruled that doughnuts can only be sold wrapped in plastic, arguing that it is demanded by the EU. It isn't.

Former Czech Prime Minister Stanislav Gross, who stepped down this April, also worked as an example of the general mood. He is only 35 years old but even when he became leader of his country, most of the foreign and European issues were not of great interest to him. His lack of interest was unfortunately visible, even during the EU summits in Brussels. It was quite clear on many occasions that he didn't know what the discussion was about; not a very good way to have influence upon important issues. This kind of bored attitude could hardly stir up the interest of many people in the country. "The European affairs are still not viewed as domestic. But they are more then ever now. Most of the things that influence lives of people in the Czech Republic happen here in Brussels. This is the place where the politics are done," says the Czech ambassador to the EU, Jan Kohout, a former member of the Convention, which was in charge of writing up the Constitution.

Shortly after joining the EU, a new challenge arrived: The European Constitution. This document is hard for most European citizens to grasp and understand. And even harder for newcomers who know even less about how the Union operates in technical and political terms, until now. It is necessary to admit that the Euro-sceptical attitude among the Czechs is, to a certain extent, overestimated. The most recent Eurobarometer poll showed that quite a comfortable majority (63%) would approve the European Constitution in the referendum. And in another poll compiled by the Czech local opinion poll agency, CVVM, in May, most of the Czechs said that the EU should have something similar to a Constitution.

Try to ask any Czech about the Constitution and the most common answer you will get is, "I do not know much about it." However, it is not just the ordinary people that have little or zero knowledge of the content of the Constitution. Even among Czech politicians, it is quite difficult to find more then a couple of dozen representatives who are able to answer basic questions regarding the Constitution, and who do not simply repeat memorised slogans about the stronger democracy (Euro-optimists) or describe the doomed journey to a new European federal state (Euro-sceptics).

But the question is: will there be any referendum? The Czech government is alone within the entire EU in that it hasn't even indicated how the Constitution will be approved: by parliament or by referendum? And here are some true political tactics that are often hard do understand. It was the opposition, mostly the Euro-sceptical ODS (Civic Democratic Party of the Czech Republic), founded by Mr Klaus, which started demanding the referendum. Originally, the party had hoped the majority of people would vote against the document. Slowly the coalition parties in the government –

all in favour of the constitutional treaty – joined in. Many pro-governmental politicians, however, criticised this decision as unnecessarily hurried.

At the beginning, it seemed too dangerous for the coalition government to hold a referendum, with first polls showing one of the lowest levels of the public being in favour. But with only a one-vote majority in the parliament it is very difficult to get the Constitution through, especially if it would be considered a constitutional change, which would require an extra 19 votes from the opposition. Government decided to simply wait and do nothing. Just recently, the Cabinet proposed a law that would anchor a general referendum in the Czech legal system, something completely unacceptable to the opposition ODS. Meanwhile, the ODS itself came up with a law establishing just a referendum on the Constitution. And we have come to a dead end, because both sides need support from each other to get their intentions through.

But it would not be Czech politics if something expected evolved. The country sank into a deep political crisis. The cabinet, led by Stanislav Gross, collapsed, and one of the parties left the coalition because of the prime minister's difficulties in explaining how he financed his luxurious flat in Prague. Meanwhile, all three political parties are back together, the cabinet is nearly the same, but Mr Gross has been replaced by his ambitious colleague, Mr Paroubek.

This political mess, which harmed the country's reputation abroad, surely did not boost the limping popularity of the centre-left government. The opposition ODS, led by Mr Mirek Topolanek, who is increasingly more pro-European then his predecessor, Vaclav Klaus, is now hoping to win the next general election in 2006 with an unprecedented majority. Having the Euro-sceptic trademark, Mr Topolanek has recently realised that many right-wing supporters dislike the ODS anti-European rhetoric. He will need these voters to create a decisive victory and prevent any new, small party making it to the parliament. Only a year ago, the Constitution was felt by the ODS to be something evil, that will do only harm. Now suddenly its politicians admit they have to take into account a risk of not approving the document by the Czech Republic.

"We are saying an optimistic, soft 'no' to the Constitution," said Mr Topolanek recently in Brussels. And the chairman of the Czech Senate, Přemysl Sobotka, has even said a soft 'yes'. Also the campaigning, which the ODS is preparing, will not be so negative after all; it should "give all the relevant information". But high-ranking members of the ODS, a party which likes to be compared to the British Conservative Party, secretly admit that it is President Klaus who does the anti-campaigning for them. Mr Klaus has become a Euro-sceptical icon in Europe, following the pattern of his model politician, the former British prime minister, Margaret Thatcher. He hasn't revealed how he voted in the referendum on the Czech entry to the EU, but he openly says an "absolute no" to the Constitution. He is the only head of state within the 25 countries with such a dismissive position. Just recently, Mr Klaus published his reasons in the Czech press for why the Constitution should be turned down. According to Mr Klaus, the document converts the Union of sovereign states into the States of Europe. He thinks the Member States will lose their right to create their own laws and, with the changes to the voting system, the Czech Republic will lose even more of its influence.

So, what do the openly pro-European parties do against this? Not much. Just recently, the cabinet decided to form a brand new department in charge of the information campaign. It will tell people what the Constitution is about and explain its positive side. But even people involved in the campaign team admit it is the toughest PR job ever. "It is hard to imagine people getting excited about the new voting system, the new president of the EU or the minister of foreign affairs," they say. And as former President Vaclav Havel pointed out, it is nonsense to hold a referendum on a document that hardly anyone has read.

In recent weeks, politicians have been more troubled with a cabinet breakdown than with the fate of the Constitution. A couple of discussions and seminars have been organised by smaller pro-European parties or Czech members of the European Parliament, and the ODS wants to use money given to it by the EPP-ED (European People's Party-European Democrats) for its own seminar, which is supposed not to be anti-Constitution. Whatever the 'new' government will do, and one of the main points of its programme is to ratify the Constitution, it will probably be President Klaus who will have the biggest influence on the public mood. According to an opinion poll published in the Mlada Fronta Dnes daily in April, most Czechs share his negative position towards the Constitution. With the government not being able to communicate its intentions to the people, it is hard to expect the public to trust what the politicians say about the document, especially when one argument is: it is important for the future of the European Union and its democracy, and the other is: the Constitution doesn't actually bring many innovative changes.

The situation has obviously dramatically changed with the rejection of the Constitution in France and the Netherlands. Even though the Czech government has always supported the Constitution, the pressure has receded and the danger that it could be just the Czech Republic that would say 'no' to the document has disappeared. The current Czech position is to continue with the ratification but, in the meantime, to have a longer deadline than October 2006. And that was the position Prime Minister Jiri Paroubek arrived in Brussels with for the EU summit. Since the European Council has decided to shelve the Constitution for at least a year, the Czech Republic has decided to delay the referendum for a further eighteen months. In the meantime, the opposition has called it a dead document and any referendum a waste of money.

It is clear that the government is either waiting for the outcome of the 'pause for reflection' or will conveniently leave the 'problem' to the next government. That could very well be the ODS, which has a strong chance of winning the next election in the spring of 2006, and which has, from the very beginning, been profoundly against the new constitutional treaty.

Hungary

During Hungary's 1,000 year-old history there have been only a few, relatively short periods of independence. This is why any attempt to limit the country's sovereignty is fraught with negative reactions among Hungarians. Still, the mood in Hungary relative to the treaty can best be described as indifferent. In fact, the ratification of the constitutional treaty went by almost unnoticed and without the Hungarians showing any interest. Their focus is not on political questions about peace, security, democracy and stability, but on economic considerations. Most of all, the EU partnership guarantees modernisation, an important element for the Hungarian people.

'Yes' To Modernisation, 'No' To Loss Of Sovereignty

by Tamás Gordon

Tamás Fóti (pen name Tamás Gordon) has been a Brussels correspondent for several Hungarian TV stations. Today he regularly publishes articles on EU and NATO issues in the national periodicals and gives lectures on EU integration issues.

A Hungarian friend, who recently visited Brussels on 'EU business', turned to me asking, "So, when is the Hungarian parliament due to vote on the EU Constitution?" Upon learning that the country actually did it months ago, (Hungary was the second country to do so, after Lithuania) he commented, "Don't take it the wrong way. I'm interested in EU matters. For example, I could tell you by heart, if you asked me, which country has yet to implement the Universal Services Directive."

His comments are a perfect illustration of the Hungarian approach to the EU Constitution. Neglectful? Hardly. The friend in question belongs to the elite and, as such, is aware of all the blessings which EU membership brings, yet at the same time does not consider the Constitution worthy of a second thought. So what can you expect from the 'average' Hungarian, who resides far from Budapest, and whose horizon doesn't necessarily go past the national border?

Throughout its stormy history, Hungary has enjoyed only short periods of freedom. Apart from the first 300 years, from the beginning of the 14th century the country was led by kings belonging to foreign royal houses, and its nobility did not speak Hungarian until the early 19th century. Hungarians tend to see themselves as the nation that saved Europe from Osmanli power, at a cost of 150 years of Turkish occupation in the 16th and 17th centuries. This also feeds the proud, national feeling of being a bastion of Christianity.

All of Hungary's attempts to regain sovereignty failed, and they were forced to accept the Hapsburg rulers. To this day, Hungarian historians continue to dispute whether the country was seen as an underdog after the failed 1848-49 freedom war when Hungary made its famous reconciliation with Austria in 1867, or was this the only way to bring about modernisation and early capitalism.

Public apathy towards the Constitution is not unique in the EU. However, the Hungarian situation is slightly different to other countries where the issue failed to trigger broad national debate. This is due to the simple fact that a large proportion of Hungarians are pro-European, and support for EU membership has not disappeared or diminished following the first year of membership. At the same time, interest towards the EU is still more for financial matters, rather than political. The only argument that counts in the public's mind is the modernisation of the country, and all the political benefits, such as stabilisation of democracy, enforcing the rule of law, etc., are of less importance.

Why? Because Hungary – and this is true for most of the region – has had a negative experience with the concept of 'integration'. Both the Warsaw Pact and Comecon (The Council for Mutual Economic Cooperation) awaken unpleasant sentiments among people here, as belonging to any alliance tends to evoke a gut reaction. But at what price? In its 1,000-year history, Hungary has enjoyed only short periods of independence, and the fall of the Berlin Wall opened the way to another chance at self-governance. Hence, any attempt to limit its political sovereignty elicits a negative reaction. As an illustration, joining NATO was always a priority for the Hungarian government, as it was for most of the established parties in the region (in parallel with EU accession) and this was looked on as a status achievement. Yet, for the public it was simply proof that the country was now saved from any potential post-Soviet influence.

Hungarians wanted the protection of NATO without the obligation of participating in what they deemed 'compromising' situations. Within two weeks of Hungary joining NATO, the country found itself at war with Yugoslavia, thus putting the Hungarian minority in that country at risk.

So, it is no wonder that one can find far more articles in the Hungarian press on the economic impact of EU membership and consequences for the budget (will the country be a net or growth contributor?) or on issues related to agriculture. At the same time, there is a dearth of information on the benefits that the tougher legislation via the EU provides in terms of cleaner air, less polluted environment – or simply the political role which the enlarged EU can play on the world stage.

In fact, throughout the work of the European Convention, the Constitution failed to materialise as a hot issue in Hungary. Some politicians tried to 'sex' it up, but merely for their party's political motives. Those who tried to emphasise the historical significance of the document had to face a mostly cynical Hungarian reaction. As a journalist noted, "Since when is it proper to refer to an infrastructure project within a Constitution?" This was in reference to the insertion of the TENs programme. (Part III, section 8 article III-246.) Frankly, it would be difficult to imagine a similar article in any national Constitution.

There was, however, one issue upon which the country's representatives, the government and the opposition found worthy of their – and the public's – attention: the collective rights of minorities. The Conservative opposition party, Fidesz, also made a case demanding a reference be made to Christianity. This is ironic if one takes into consideration that the party was, after the fall of communism, the most radical and anti-clerical in the country, and it only resorted to populist politics and nationalist tendencies because of an insatiable appetite for power.

Less exciting, but still garnering a certain degree of interest was the fact that Hungary would be able to keep its Commissioner in the European Commission until at least 2014. The 'personalisation' of one of the most important EU institutions is something which could illicit a positive reaction from the public, largely because the political elite failed to point out that the Commissioner is – at least on paper – independent from the government, and is not in Brussels to represent his/her country's interest but rather to act exclusively at the European level. This misconstruing of roles explains the government's energetic lobbying to postpone the rotation system of a limited number of Commissioners for as long as possible. At the adoption of the Constitution in Brussels in June 2004, the then prime minister, Péter Medgyessy, claimed that to please Hungarian demand, the Council had agreed that even after 2014 (the earliest opportunity to change the composition of the Commission) it would still be possible to continue with the 'one country – one Commissioner' policy. This was a slight deviation from the facts, because to change the commitment to reduce the number of Commissioners to two thirds of the total members, the Council would have to come to a unanimous decision.

When Hungary (regardless of which international stage is in discussion) raises the issue of minority rights, it by no means refers to minorities living in the country. Rather, its focus is on the *Hungarian* minorities residing in neighbouring countries; some three million Hungarians live in Slovakia, Ukraine, Romania and Serbia. For more than half a century, their fate has been the subject of constant tension between Hungary and the surrounding region. During the work of the Convention, the Hungarian representatives tried hard to insert into the text a guarantee for the collective rights of minorities. After recognising that this would likely require a compromise on their part, the government submitted a clause on minorities that accepted that the Union values, among others, "the respect for human rights including the rights of persons belonging to minorities".

The wording found its way into the text in Article 1-2: "The Union is founded on the values of respect for human dignity, liberty, democracy, equality, the rule of law, and respect for human rights including the rights of persons belonging to minorities." The Hungarian delegation argued it was absurd and unacceptable that among the Copenhagen criteria there was a mention of the "respect for and protection of minorities", but that once a state was 'inside' the EU, those criteria ceased to exist.

There was no mention of a specific minority clause in the EU Charter of Fundamental Rights adopted by the Council in Nice in 2000. The draft EU Constitution, completed on 10 July 2003 by the EU Convention on the future of Europe, was equally silent on the rights of minorities. The formulation in the draft Constitution sent the wrong message that the minority clause served as a specific requirement only during accession procedures, and that after enlargement the EU no longer considered it worthwhile to call attention to it. In the end, Hungary achieved only a partial success; the text refers to the individual rights of minorities. This is still considered a great achievement given the sensitivity surrounding the whole issue, particularly in France, which for a long time fought vehemently against the Hungarian proposition.

The question of whether there should be a reference to God has never been considered by the government to be an important issue. The official position, however, has changed periodically to reflect domestic perception of the issue. While Hungarian society was for the most part apathetic on the theme – there were no wide discussions about it – the opposition saw its chance to formulate an attack against the government, as part of its *Kulturkampf*. The government reluctantly accepted the bait, stating that even though a reference to God was not a priority, Hungary was nevertheless ready to use it as a 'bargaining card'.

The government's position was that it supported all the ideas of other countries provided it did not hurt national interest and, in exchange, the country in question would also support the Hungarian demand. For a long period, this was the case with Poland, which fought desperately for a reference to God, but in the last round of negotiations, the Hungarian government chose to 'forget' about the deal and was happy with the universal reference to religion, which remains in the Constitution today.

The idea behind the change of heart concerning Poland can be found in the fact that for Budapest it was vital to get assent from Paris on the minority question and, to secure it, it was necessary to support the French government's demand to omit any reference to God in the Preamble. Furthermore, the government supported the idea to end the right of veto in most fields. However, it insisted on maintaining this right in two spheres: culture and defence policy. But these are not particularly Hungarian issues so upon securing them, the government had the comfortable position of being able to lie back in the last phase of the 'fight'.

The ratification process went relatively unnoticed, with no significant discussion in parliament. Within the civil society, there was only one communiqué from the Hungarian Europe Society (HES), which outlined why there was no need for a referendum in Hungary. Incidentally, even this lone reaction went unnoticed. The HES argued that a referendum on the accession to the EU had only recently occurred. Indeed, there was an overwhelming majority favouring membership, but with a very low voter turnout of only 45.6 %, due to the fact that the no-camp barely existed. The disappointing turnout led the HES to conclude that if even a referendum on EU membership failed to mobilise public interest, a vote on the Constitution – an issue that had received far less coverage – was likely to be even lower. This could have been misinterpreted as a disinterest towards the EU as a whole.

During the ratification discussion in the parliament there was one representative, an MEP, who used the same argument as to why there was no need for a referendum. He stated that in 2003, 80% of those who voted were in favour of accession and in 2004, during the European parliamentary elections, the pro-EU parties received 90 % of the votes.

After observing the turbulent campaigns in certain Member States, long after Hungary's ratification of the Constitution in December 2004, the Hungarian branch of the leftist anti-globalisation movement, ATTAC, issued a communiqué. In its congratulations to the French no-camp, it stated, "We condemn in our country the parliament's ratification of the

Constitution without any public debate, by politicians serving the interests of those with economic power."[28]

In contrast to this statement, the above-mentioned Hungarian Europe Society (HES) initiated a new campaign for a Europe-wide referendum whose goal was to save the Constitution. Only a year ago, the HES was opposed to even a single Hungarian referendum saying, "The time has not yet come for a European-wide referendum, because we have yet to reach the point where its result would be accepted throughout the Union…"). Today it proposes an all-European referendum according to the principle of the double majority, detailed in Article I-25 of the Constitution.

The HES's argument is simple: the double 'no' in two of the founding Member States, weakened the faith for a "common European idea". In order to regain it and assist in the adoption of the Constitution, the best way would be to hold a Europe-wide referendum. What is the logic in holding it simultaneously in all Member States? That the victory of the no-camps had little to do with the Constitution itself? Therefore "the questions would have arisen in a European perspective for the French and the Dutch people as well, had each EU citizen eligible to vote had the opportunity to formulate his/her decision concerning the Constitution on a Europe-wide level". To bring this proposition to fruition, the HES began collecting signatures (following the spirit of the Constitution – Article I-47 paragraph 4).

The 'official' Hungarian reaction to the result of the two referendums was restricted to a statement by the Hungarian Prime Minister, Ferenc Gyurcsány, who said that since its establishment in 1957, the European Union now faces its biggest challenge following the two referendums, and "one cannot forecast the consequences". The Hungarian parties handed the field over to their MEPs, who mainly followed the lines of their political groups within the European Parliament. Weeks after the Dutch 'no', the Hungarian socialist MEPs, having received the assent of the mother party (Hungarian Socialist Party, MSZP), announced a major countrywide campaign for autumn 2005 with the slogan: "We are Europe". Its goal is to make Hungarians familiar with the EU. However, given that the lack of public awareness on the EU is not unique to Hungary, one cannot help but suspect that the motive behind this initiative is directly related to MSZP's campaign ahead of the 2006 spring parliamentary elections.

One of the main architects of Hungary's accession to the EU told me in a private conversation that the Constitution is no more than a compilation of the codification of all EU legislation. He expressed his doubts as to whether the document could make any revolutionary achievement. Going further, he

---

[28] See www.attac.hu

blamed Giscard d'Estaing and several individuals from his circle for establishing their own ideas and claimed that no one can speak about a real Constitution. His opinion reflects and explains well the lukewarm activity by the Hungarian government during the IGC and its minimal communication on the matter to the Hungarian public.

Conclusion

Four Steps Towards A More Promising European Collaboration – With Popular Support

by Anders Samuelsen (translated by Helen Bang)

Europe has achieved a great deal. On 12 July 2005, when the British chancellor of the exchequer, visited the European Parliament, he summarised its achievements so far:

> *Since the Second World War, we have moved from war to peace. We have tamed the market forces, and introduced a market economy built on strong welfare states. We have expanded the European collaboration to include Eastern Europe, and most recently at the G8 summit in July, the EU helped put Africa on the agenda through debt-relief. We have much to be proud of.*

Or – as has correctly been pointed out – judged by the daily output of journalists, Europe is in a perpetual state of crisis. But judged by the wider criteria of historians, the EU is a global historical success without comparison – as an institution, as a creator of welfare, and as an engine for the development of new democracies – and not through violence or force, but by setting an example and being a club, entry to which is still sought after by many countries.

However, Gordon Brown did point out that Europe is in a state of crisis. Twenty million Europeans are without a job and European countries are not equipped to deal with the change in the world's economy from national and regional to global. Plenty needs to be done.

From reading the 15 chapters of this book, it is clear that Europe has reached a crossroads. Either we proudly continue, limping along the same old track, or else we face reality and conclude that some changes are necessary. It would be easiest to continue as though nothing had happened, and to try one day to resurrect the Constitution.

We can rejoice in all that we actually have achieved. As Gordon Brown confirms, the EU is unquestionably Europe's greatest achievement since the Second World War.

It is tempting to rest on our laurels: the institutions have been built, the parliament continues to operate, legislation is passed, initiatives proposed, meetings held and so on. Even crises will not split the EU. Cleverly built networks and institutions ensure against its downfall. All of this is in keeping with the spirit of Jean Monnet, one of the chief architects of the Union, but it is not a sustainable strategy for the future. Three central EU countries, the Netherlands, Germany and France, are plagued by high unemployment, low economic growth and a mistrust of their political leaders.

The facts speak for themselves. Europe is facing some big challenges, and the nation states cannot tackle them alone. We need a strong and reformed EU providing a framework for the contributions of the nation states, a framework that can ensure a tempo and development that reflects the desires of the people. This does not happen by itself.

There is a need for concrete action. The 15 chapters of this book testify to the need to modernise the EU, the need to deal with certain absurdities and taboos, and set ambitious objectives. In the end, the debate was not about the details of the constitutional treaty, or about the greater values that are supposed to bring us together. Below I will outline four steps for developing the EU in certain areas, while limiting it in others, and I hope these will simultaneously create support for the project.

Step One: Combating crime

The issue of security has always held a prominent place in EU history. The EU was founded to avoid another French/German war, and then the east/west conflict took centre stage. Today terrorism and crime across borders are on the agenda.

Especially in an age of terror, it becomes clear that there are tasks which single countries are unable to complete alone. As long as international networks are committing crime and terrorism across borders, there will be a need for collaboration across borders to combat this. Ad hoc collaboration is not enough. We need commitment. Long-term collaboration will make a difference, not quick efforts based on terrible events.

Institutionally, police collaboration exists directly between national police authorities and through Europol. The collaboration is particularly concerned with preventing and fighting organised crime and, increasingly, fighting terrorism. Collaboration also takes place directly between the relevant authorities of the Member States, as well as through Eurojust (a cooperative venture between Member States' prosecutors).

One of the current initiatives being discussed on how to combat terror is common European laws on retaining data from phone calls and e-mail traffic. The United Kingdom, Ireland, Sweden and France would like to see common EU laws in this area. Following the terror attacks in London, the support of the proposal will most likely increase. Another initiative focuses on the more effective targeting of the economy which finances terror, including money laundering. After the attacks on London, it is being proposed that we carry a European ID card with so-called biometric indicators, which are distinctive marks unique to the individual such as fingerprints and scans of the iris. To ensure increased safety with travel documents it has already been agreed that from August 2006 biometric passports containing fingerprints and digital photos will be introduced.

Combating terror is not the only area where it makes sense to work together. Drugs crime, financial crime, human trafficking and illegal immigration are other obvious issues that would benefit from increased collaboration. In fighting these types of crime, central European crime records have been considered. The crime records could also be beneficial in the combating of paedophilia. Without the central records, a convicted paedophile could move from France to Belgium where he could continue his misdeeds because the police collaboration between the countries was not strong enough to stop him. The situation may have been different had the police in France and Belgium had on-line access to a European database of convictions. However, such a register invites criticism. How do we control who has access to these convictions and should the register include information on all crime, including simple theft? Until now, it has not been possible to reach an agreement at EU level regarding centralised European criminal records, with the result that Belgium, France and Spain trilaterally continue to work on an electronic exchange of convictions between the countries.

As is apparent, the EU could cooperate in fighting crime in many ways. The collaboration on this issue is greatly supported by the European populations, but the common commitment is not without its problems. It is significantly problematic that the Member States do not always include EU law in their national law. One example of this is the European warrant, which ensures that people living in an EU country can be extradited to and prosecuted in another EU country for crimes committed there. The European warrant should have been introduced on 1 January 2004, but Italy did not make the necessary changes until May 2005. This shows that inefficiency in fighting terror is not always due to absent legislation but due to Member States' slow implementation of EU legislation at a national level. It is simply not good enough.

Another important consideration is that our liberal rights are not put under too much strain. Finding the right balance is a huge and fundamental task.

Surveillance and recording can give a greater sense of security, but may also reduce our freedom. Take, for example, the suggested recording of each e-mail sent or every phone call made. We are left with many unanswered questions. Is it only the sender, receiver and time that are to be recorded? Will this ever change to include content? One thing is certain: as long as Al-Qaeda and Eastern European thieves work across borders, an EU coordination seems sensible. But again, we must find the right balance. The initiatives we pass to fight terror must not undermine our democracy and respect for the rights of the individual. It is these rights that we are aiming to protect.

So far, in Denmark, we have been reticent with regard to surveillance. The nightmare vision is one of a Big Brother society where freedom is dramatically curtailed by government control. But is surveillance really this frightening? Opposition to video surveillance is seemingly weaker in the population than amongst politicians. Many citizens feel unsafe in half-empty trains late at night. To them, a greater sense of safety and security weighs heavier than theoretical considerations about Big Brother. One could interject that video surveillance is no guarantee against terror – the terror attacks on London happened despite heavy surveillance. Nevertheless, the British police were able to identify the suspects immediately through CCTV recordings. Even though surveillance may not have a preventative function, it can help to solve the case. Yet again, we must ask ourselves how far we are willing to go and with which tools we can equip our police and judicial system to prevent crime and punish criminals. In my opinion, the Danes need to be less sceptical of video surveillance as a means to combat crime. The conclusion is that there is a need for more intensive cooperation, more surveillance, and more sharing of data.

Step Two: A new way to enlargements

The enlargement of the EU has been an unbelievably democratic process. Europe has been healed in record time, and millions of Europeans are now joined in peaceful co-existence. Unfortunately, we must admit that the process of enlargement has been put under pressure by the rejections in France and the Netherlands. Among the explanations offered for this setback are dissatisfaction with the speed of the enlargements so far and the prospect of more to come, in particular with Turkey. Turkey's possible accession is the most controversial of all, and I will therefore deal with it here in extension. Many inhabitants fear losing influence and jobs to new Member States with lower wages. They feel threatened by globalisation and perceive enlargement as part of the problem and not part of the solution. This is a worry we must take seriously.

The French have been promised a referendum on the inclusion of Turkey and it looks as though there will also be a referendum in Austria. At the same time, the latest opinion polls show that it would take an extraordinary effort to create public support for the inclusion of Turkey.

I believe that the EU has much to gain if Turkey changes enough to become a full member in the future, in terms of both security issues and finance.

It is imperative that we support the reformers, who wish to follow the European path, and at the same time weaken the fundamentalists, who seek isolation and confrontation. Islam is not the enemy. Fundamentalists – Christian, Muslim or whatever they may be – constitute the problem. Turkey should be included in the political cooperation, in fact the country should be embraced.

Opposed to this line of thought is a massive public scepticism. Whilst sad, it is nevertheless a fact that demands to be heeded by change. We will not satisfactorily resolve the question of Turkey, or any questions that arise with regard to possible future enlargements, or make any headway with a new treaty unless we create a sense of security surrounding the process that may lead to Turkey's future membership. However unfair it may seem, the potential for political unrest caused by the 'Polish plumber' is nothing compared to the potential for conflicts caused by the (Muslim) Turkish lower paid workers.

Therefore, we must be clear. The process of admission by which Turkey may hopefully one day gain membership must not to be a repeat of earlier admission processes. This does not mean that we need to invent new demands for Turkey, but we must adhere to the demands we have made and find a new model for admission, a model which takes into account that it will be a longer process, and that the risk of Turkey achieving something other than full membership is greater than has been the case with recent admissions.

A new admission model must have three objectives. It must retain the real possibility of Turkey becoming a member whilst removing any suspicion of an automatic process. It must gradually tie Turkey closer to Europe as the country progresses. Finally, it must ensure that there is full public support if the EU and Turkey are one day to accept each other.

The EU must demand 100% compliance with the Copenhagen Criteria.[29] This must be done in deeds as well as words. There can be no case, as has

---

[29] In 1993, the European Council in Copenhagen agreed on a number of demands, which must be complied with by countries that apply for membership. The three main criteria concern

happened previously, for giving discounts. It can seem unfair to tighten the rules now but the task is greater than in any previous enlargement and not tightening the rules will in no way benefit the EU or Turkey. Any story relaying how Turkey does not live up to the Copenhagen Criteria will only make it more difficult to convince politicians and the public of the benefits of Turkish membership. The EU commission seems to have begun tightening the rules, but there is a major task in explaining to the public what the Copenhagen Criteria actually mean. It must be made crystal-clear that it will be a different Turkey from today which can eventually join the EU.

We need to challenge the idea that there is no return once admission negotiations have commenced. This is the case whether Turkey achieves full membership or not. The people of the EU and Turkey will see (as in the recent case of Croatia) that an inability to meet the demands of the EU will have immediate consequences.

In addition to full compliance with the Copenhagen Criteria and the introduction of so-called doorstops, we also need a 'step-by-step' model. In other words, a 'mutual legitimacy' test that involves a very gradual assimilation of Turkey – step-by-step – and at a pace which Turkey and the rest of Europe can maintain. Even more so than with previous enlargements, we need to think in phases. The aim is not the creation of a privileged partnership, but it nevertheless makes sense to give Turkey some kind of privileged status in a number of areas during the process towards possible full membership. As mentioned above, further integration must happen at a pace Turkey and Europe can keep up with – neither faster, nor slower.

The Commission is already moving in the right direction when it comes to phased admissions. Today, the EU collaborates with Turkey on research and exchange programmes for students. Turkey fully participates in the Socrates exchange programme for students and the Jean Monnet programme for researchers is currently being improved.[30]

There is no reason to rest here. As soon as possible, Turkey must be included in the common foreign and security policies, and also receive infrastructural support from the EU. The current Customs Union must expand to include Turkey in the inner market, with the exception of the free movement of labour. But Turkey should not to be included in EU agricultural policies, the Cohesion Fund, or the Solidarity Fund in order to

---

democracy (democratic electoral processes, abiding by human rights and respect of minorities), finance (liberal competitive market and the ability to compete with other EU countries), and administration (willingness and ability to follow EU legislation, and the ideas behind the founding of the EU).

[30] For a detailed description, see the Commission's paper: Civil Society Dialogue between the EU and Candidate Countries, June 2005.

achieve economic harmonisation. However, it would seem obvious to give Turkey special status in the cooperation of combating crime across borders and tackling illegal immigration. In the same way that Norway currently partakes in the Schengen collaboration on open borders, it is possible that in 10-15 years, prior to membership, it will make sense to do away with border inspections between Turkey and the EU, at least provisionally.[31]

This will send a signal to the Turkish people that they are a part of Europe and the EU population will not perceive that the open borders constitute a threat. At the same time, it is important to make clear that it will be many years before we open up to free movement of labour. Whether the free movement of labour ought to precede a possible full membership or follow it in the process of a longer and more gradual absorption (such as we have seen from our most recent enlargements towards the Eastern European countries) is too early to say.

Finally, in a few years time, Turkish politicians must be allowed to participate as observers at European summits and at the European Parliament's sessions, with the right to speak but not to vote. This will jump start the dialogue and support the Turkish reformists wishing to bring the country closer to the EU.

As a whole, Turkey's involvement will increase, although the country will only participate in areas that affect approximately 40% of the EU budget.

Following several years of implementation according to this model, both parties in the assimilation process will have had time to assess each other.

In principle, I am opposed to holding referendums about other countries' populations. But given the particularly problematic situation with Turkey, we should consider ending the accession process with a joint European referendum. It is entirely possible that a joint referendum in perhaps fifteen years has a good chance of rendering a majority at a European level. Today there is a majority in favour of Turkey in countries such as Spain, Poland and the United Kingdom, but the feeling of not being heard can quickly lead to opposition as seen in the referendums in France and the Netherlands.

If Turkey succeeds in improving its image considerably through real and massive progress – which Turkey must do to have a chance of joining the EU – a concluding referendum will strengthen the public support to the idea

---

[31] When travelling in another Schengen country, one must be in possession of a passport or another type of valid travel documentation. This easier access to travel does not provide access to social benefits or permission to work. The Schengen collaboration involves broad and intimate collaboration between the police and the tax authorities.

of a Turkish membership. In addition, one has to wonder if the EU can even survive admitting Turkey if more than 50% of the European populations as a whole is opposed.

The aim of this new model for enlargement is to avoid the situation where politicians find themselves desperately trying to convince suspicious populations. The process must be considered safe from the outset. Otherwise opposition will grow and the process will either lose tempo dramatically, or come to a halt altogether, handing success to the opponents of Turkey's inclusion to the severe detriment of both future applicant countries and the present members of the union.

If the population is convinced that Turkey is meeting the demands of a fully democratic country, and it is apparent that the collaboration works in certain other areas, then it will be possible to create a majority in favour. According to a Danish opinion poll,[32] we know that the population's views are varied. When asked the question "Do you think that Turkey should be admitted into the EU?" the majority replied "No". However, when asked whether Turkey should be able to be a member when the country has implemented the necessary reforms they say "Yes". The response is determined by the way in which the question is framed, and the Danish figures indicate that support for Turkish membership is possible if we create a new model for admission.

Step Three: Remove the absurdities and make the cooperation meaningful

The European collaboration must no longer accept that every discussion is sidetracked by pure idiocy. Repeatedly, those of us who support the EU point out that European administration costs are minor compared to national administration costs. However, our arguments fade in the light of the EU's few but grotesque injustices. A ready example is the monthly travelling between Brussels and Strasbourg, when, due to national interests, politicians and colleagues must leave Belgium for four days to work in France. The arrangement is so absurd that it defies every description, and causes wholly understandable indignation. It is therefore easy to shrug your shoulders, and ask: if this sort of thing is acceptable, what it isn't?

The arrangement must be abolished. It is symbolic of the EU being driven by national private interests. If politicians defend such a system, how can they be perceived as trustworthy when they present ideas for growth in Europe? Moreover, they are not trusted, and with good reason. The EU does

---

[32] Seven out of ten Danes agree with the statement that at some point in the future Turkey ought to become a member of the EU on condition that the country implements the most necessary political and financial reforms. Source: Danish Industry, January 2005.

not have the means to activate attractive objectives, mainly as the money is being spent in the wrong areas. Travelling to Strasbourg does not make a huge dent in the budget but there are two other absurdities with very different consequences that we must consider, if for no other reason than in order for us to be able to invest in other areas: farm subsidies and the British rebate.

The two agreements are defended on historical grounds, which expired long ago. No matter how we look at it, there is no reason to sustain our current levels of farm subsidies. The taxpayers of the EU are financing an open-air museum. The result is a distorted market, which prejudices commercial interests in the poorer countries. Today Europe's agriculture is an industry like any other and it must survive on the conditions of the market. We do not clog factories for nostalgic reasons – they have had to become self-sufficient or sell out. The subsidies should be phased out quickly and efficiently, though at a pace which is fair to that 5% of the European population that lives in agricultural areas. The state of emergency present after the Second World War no longer prevails, and we no longer lack groceries. In fact, we are faced with an obesity epidemic.

Among others, France benefits greatly from agricultural aid. Because of this, the UK has retained its own cash cow, the British rebate on their yearly contribution to EU. The discount was negotiated by Margaret Thatcher who showily declared: "I want my money back!" She got it, but when the agricultural subsidies disappear, it will no longer be possible to defend the rebate. Let us take Tony Blair at his word and reveal what is spin and what is fact in his claims that the UK will relinquish the rebate if farm subsidies are put on the agenda. Should we succeed, we will kill two birds with one stone and increase our investment means many times over.

Following the adjustment to the excesses of the EU and its two parliaments, the abolition of farm subsidies and the British rebate, we shall have more means with which to operate. This must be divided into areas, which make sense in a globalised world. Here again we need to look at the relation between the EU and its Member States. We must decide upon the areas we wish to prioritise, and then on how to divide the workload between the EU and its constituent members.

The Organisation for European Co-operation and Development (OECD) recently published a set of alarming figures on the growth of the EU. The EU needs to implement fundamental reforms and investments in the coming years otherwise the entire EU growth from 2020-2030 will not reach 3% per annum (as stipulated by the Lisbon strategy) but only 1%. By contrast, the US is expected to maintain its growth of over 3%.[33]

In 2004, the EU spent 0.3% of its budget investing in research, 0.3% on environmental implementations, 1.1% on developing energy and transport, 0.9% on education and culture, and 0.4% on health and consumer interests. In comparison, we spend 49.4% on agriculture and 22.1% on regional politics.[34] The disproportion is obvious.

However, the potential too is obvious. The EU can expect a stronger public mandate if it reforms the budget and the collaboration starts affecting areas in the public interest. People must sense that the EU makes a real and positive difference when it turns to deal with problems close to their own hearts.[35]

Primarily this means creating new jobs and ensuring financial growth, as well as fighting crime and improvements on health and environmental matters. Though it may not be a daily concern for the public, they still believe that the EU guarantees peace and security in Europe. The EU's function as peacemaker is a crucial area for further progress.

The issue now is how to divide the areas of contribution between the EU and the Member States. It is not possible to do this in an entirely strict way, since new challenges demand new kinds of collaboration. Supranational regulation of telecommunications and energy was hardly necessary 40 years ago, but today it makes sense. Common rules for the use of chemicals were unnecessary prior to industrialisation but today, for example, we need to prohibit hormonally destabilising chemicals in bath toys across the borders. And so it goes on. New problems need new answers. However, we can present two principles in the division of labour between the EU and the Member States: The principles of subsidiarity and large-scale operations. The principle of subsidiarity is well known and aims at making decisions close to the Member State because it makes sense. I propose to complement this principle with the principle of large-scale operations: we must make common financial investments when it can be shown that the benefits are greater than the investment at a national level. In other words, the EU must

---

[33] OECD: Economic Survey of the Euro Area, July 2005.

[34] The European Union's general budget for 2004 according to the European Commission, 2003.

[35] When asked, 50% of the population of the EU say that unemployment constitutes the biggest problem for their country. Next comes the economic situation (27%), followed by crime (23%), the health service (17%), inflation (16%), immigration (14%), pensions (11%), terrorism (10%), taxes (7%), education (7%), environmental protection (4%) public transport (2%) and defence and security (2%). Source: The EU Commission: Standard Eurobarometer 63, July 2005.

be the favoured vehicle in cases where there is an obvious pay-off for operations of a larger scale.

Following this principle, we should prioritise the EU's efforts into three areas in particular: research and education; health and environmental issues, and foreign and security policy.

Research and education

If we heed the recommendations of the OECD, it seems obvious to prioritise further joint investment in education and research. Out of the 20 best universities in the world, only two (Cambridge and Oxford) are situated in Europe and this is not acceptable. In addition to national universities, the EU must invest in the creation of top universities in five or six areas of Europe.

By placing further education within a European framework, we can increase standards significantly. This applies equally to investment in research. We must continue to make the majority of our research contributions at a national level but it makes sense to pick certain areas for cross-national EU investments, for example research into cancer or alternative sources of energy. In chosen areas, the EU must gather the highest expertise to work in an optimum research environment. It does not make sense for all Member States to undertake separate but parallel research in the same areas. The result will be a levelling-out between Member States. The EU will never become the United States of Europe, but we would consider it a pointless investment if each of the states in the USA invested in research separately and did not pool the investment. It is equally pointless in Europe when we fail to gather our expertise in optimum research centres. At research level, it is plain that we will reap a greater benefit when investing on a collaborative, as opposed to a national, level.

Environment and health

Alongside the implementation of the common market, the EU has introduced legislation on safety, health, and environmental issues. The aim was to tame the market forces for the benefit of the people. The first area in need of investment was the environment. It was pointless to limit national air pollution when neighbouring countries let their poisonous emissions float over their borders. In other words, common initiatives were beneficial. On environmental issues, Denmark has worked to ensure tighter regulations in all Member States and the next challenge will be the new legislation on chemicals, or REACH. There is a clear need for a common tightening of the rules, and Denmark will continue to pioneer protection of the environment and consumers.

The EU countries are experienced in working closely together on environmental issues, but we are less intimate when it comes to our health services, and prefer to invest locally. However, there is much to be gained from common investment in this area. In recent years, we have seen great progress in the treatment of many illnesses and are expecting great breakthroughs in the treatment of cancer. This is a very positive development but it does present some dilemmas. As we develop more medicines and procedures, we are able to treat more patients who were previously diagnosed as incurably ill. More patients are treatable, and the life expectancy of Danes is on the rise due to general health improvements. This is naturally a pleasing development, but it is also expensive. The cost of the health budget is rising, with the result that we are unable to give everyone the best available treatment. This gives rise to difficult and uncomfortable medico-ethical questions such as: Do we focus on the treatment of widespread diseases whilst giving rare diseases less priority? Do we not treat very old patients? Do we treat the 'best' patients first, i.e. patients who have a higher chance of recovery due to good general health, rather than patients who are obese, who smoke or consume large amounts of alcohol? These are all tricky questions to ask in the public and political arena. They involve ethical and moral dilemmas, which are difficult to master. However, they will soon become a pressing reality. Doctors are already facing some of these questions because we as politicians have avoided the issue.

We cannot and must not avoid the debate, and we will have to prioritise. Prioritising on the public budget will be a more human exercise if we can pool our investments through the EU, and gather our expertise at various centres across Europe. We cannot afford to offer the best treatment to all patients in each of the 25 Member States. However, one could imagine being able to offer the best treatment for a rare disease such as cystic fibrosis in Munich, whilst some of the best surgeons on breast cancer are gathered in Paris or Stockholm, and the most talented heart surgeons are in Copenhagen, and so on. All these are hypothetical examples and they all demand practical challenges of huge proportions, and offer great potential.

One obvious impediment is that patients would naturally prefer to be treated in their own local environment. No one wishes to leave a safe and familiar place at a time of illness and uncertainty. However, I believe most patients would prefer to travel 1,000 or 1,500 kilometres to be operated on by a surgeon who daily performs the type of operation needed, rather than going under the knife at a local hospital that performs the operation once every six months. Let us explore the possibilities before necessity takes over.

Foreign and security policy

Finally, it is obvious that we need to increase our investment in security. During the build up to the war in Iraq, it became apparent how small a role the EU plays in the politics of international security. All Member States voiced their views independently, with the result that the signals from the EU were contradictory. This can of course be defended on the basis that in foreign policy there were no simple answers and truths. Foreign policy is difficult, particularly difficult as it touches on death and survival, freedom and repression. Each decision is of crucial importance, as are even those that are not made – as in the case of the break-up of the former Yugoslavia. Had we intervened quickly and decisively after the first shots had been fired, much death and destruction could have been avoided. But Europe was at a loss, and it is not surprising that the US failed to take the EU's message seriously when it came to Iraq, since there were too many views.

We need to decide on what are the EU's aims in the wider world. Until then we rely too much on the shelter of the US and on the bad excuse that 'it's the UN's responsibility'. Remember our weakness in the former Yugoslavia, and in relation to Rwanda, Darfur, Congo, Iraq, Iran, and so on. We are simply not trustworthy, and can certainly not live up to the motto: "speak softly and carry a big stick".

The lesson is that the EU must speak with one voice, not to become a second super power, but in order to play an important role to supplement to the USA's dominance. Otherwise, the world will too often find itself between an incompetent Europe with many worthy ideals, and a US that does as it pleases. The constitutional treaty was partly aimed at ensuring this. The treaty introduces a common foreign minister and we must pursue this. CFSP – the EU's common foreign and security policy – is vital for Europe's activities in the world at large. Only an EU with larger and better-coordinated investments can function as a critic of and player with the US. The CFSP must be pursued as a matter of priority. If, during this process, we can prepare ourselves to deal with future conflicts as the relations to the Third World (sidelined until now) then we will have begun to create something of meaning – not just for the political elite, but for the people of Europe.

Step Four: A deep sigh – stop the untrustworthy campaigns

We all know that peace and freedom are not to be taken for granted. We know that it is not a matter of course that Europe does not stand in flames as it did during the Second World War. We know that not everyone enjoys freedom of speech, freedom of conscience and rights of assembly. That said, politicians must realise that this knowledge does not guarantee public support for the EU itself. If this were the case, the French and the Dutch would not have rejected the constitutional treaty. But they did. Not because they are ungrateful or ignorant of the EU's role in maintaining peace and stability. But why? As seen in the chapter on referendums, the yes-camp has shown itself to be its own worst enemy in campaign situations. As soon as the yes-camp start campaigning, they take a hit in the polls. The yes-camp make lavish promises, including cheap goods, reduced unemployment and low interest rates. However, it is not that simple. Although Ireland, Portugal and Spain have experienced great progress, and although the Eastern European countries have high growth rates, there is still unemployment and social inequality, even in those countries which have been most successful.

In Denmark, the threat was that a rejection of the euro would bring high interest rates and increased unemployment. This did not happen, and those who spoke up for the euro in this way have thereby lost credit. Similarly, many Dutch, Italians and Germans are convinced today that the cost of their groceries did not come down when they entered the euro, and that these costs have in fact increased. During the debate on the constitutional treaty, the Dutch people did not believe their government's claim that European countries would break out in war were the treaty rejected. In fact, this claim only increased their defiance and mistrust. There are many reasons behind the fate of the treaty, but one thing is for certain: scare tactics do not work. On the contrary, they promote the case of the opponent. This is also the case for the many golden promises. Voters simply do not believe in them.

So give up the untrustworthy campaigns and be honest about the contributions. Focus on what we believe we can gain from the treaty and initiatives but leave threats and unsubstantiated promises by the wayside.

And if the no-camp would be so kind as to do the same. Give up the threats about the end of the nations, the birth of the United States of Europe, the over-zealous Brussels and much more, then the way might actually be paved to let the citizens and the possibilities take centre stage.

But is the agenda outlined above realistic? To expect to rid the EC of its absurdities, to re-jig the budget, to invest in research, consumer protection and new workplaces, to battle terror and adopt a common foreign policy. Is this not too naïve or unrealistic? No one can predict with certainty how the EU will develop in the coming years. The idea of my proposals is simply to point out what seems to me to be necessary. Here are some comments on some of the possibilities.

Nothing is as it used to be. This point is best illustrated by my own first experience in the European Parliament, which was of the case of the Italian candidate for the Commission, Rocco Buttiglione. Every experienced commentator and politician in and around the chamber shrugged their shoulders when the Parliament threatened to reject the homophobic and misogynistic Commissioner. A Danish colleague was certain enough to offer me a wager: "I have seen it so often, Anders. Initially the Parliament puffs out its chest, then the home country speaks in capital letters, and we all end up coming to heel."

But as we all know, this did not happen. Everything was not as it used to be. The recently elected Parliament was constituted of enough new politicians from new Member States that things were no longer so predictable.

Since then, things have become even less predictable – not least following the debate (or lack of debate) on the constitutional treaty.

The chance to make fundamental change, although not great, is nevertheless greater than ever. The predictability and the old balance of power disappeared when France and the Netherlands rejected the treaty, with the polls showing that the Germans would have rejected it had they been given the chance to vote. Dissatisfaction with unemployment, financial crisis, and lack of political leadership were important reasons behind the two rejections; the populations did not believe that they were offered a credible strategy for the future.

This signal has now been picked up by even the most tone-deaf politicians. One of the politicians most in tune with the desires of the public, Tony Blair, has suggested a thorough change in the politics of the EU. Great Britain would shift the economy away from agriculture towards a huge investment in research and development. The EU is to make a noticeable difference on areas such as employment, health, and the environment. No matter what people say of Blair's engagement in Europe, he is one of the most efficient of the continent's leaders. There is support behind the reform of farm subsidies and getting away from thinking in grooves. Reform will be toned down but the process has begun, and many years earlier than even the most optimistic among us had expected.

Add to this that two of Europe's old bigwigs, Jacques Chirac and Gerhard Schröder, have initiated and experienced domestic political depression, and will both possibly soon be replaced by forces more supportive of change. In France, the Minister of Interior, Nicolas Sarkozy, has already pointed out that the purely Franco-German alliance is old hat, and that his vision of Europe bears more resemblance to Great Britain's (*The Guardian*, 6 July 2005). In Germany, the conservative Angela Merkel is ready to take over from Schröder – at least that is the prediction from the early stages of the election campaign. Her European politics are close to Blair's and the support from France and Germany adds to that of the Eastern European countries of the EU. If they are guaranteed not to lose out in the far-reaching budget reforms, they will support Blair's ideas. The Nordic countries also see the need for decreasing farm subsidies and prioritising research, education, and development. In other words, change is not a utopian vision.

European politics are in ferment. We must seize the opportunity.

Appendix

A Brief Introduction To The Constitutional Treaty:

The aim of the constitutional treaty is to ensure a more efficient and decisive EU following the enlargement to 25 countries. The treaty codifies the EU's earlier treaties into a unifying text that clarifies how the EU is made up, what its powers are, and which goals and ideals lie beneath the European collaboration. It is important to underline the following six points:

Clear division of tasks

The Constitution simplifies the European project and creates a clearer distribution of responsibilities between the EU and its Member States. If the Constitution had been agreed, the responsibilities of the EU and its Member States would have been clearer. The treaty defines when and in which areas the EU has single and/or shared responsibility, as well as when it should coordinate or supplement the investments of its members.

Greater authority to the European Parliament

The Constitution more than doubles the political areas in which the EU must govern through a common decision-making procedure. The procedure aligns the Council of Ministers with the European Parliament. Agreeing the Constitution would have ensured that the European Parliament passes bills on 73% of political areas before they become EU laws. This would have meant a significant expansion of Parliament's influence.

Simpler decision-making procedures

The Constitution proposes new and comprehensible rules on a qualified majority in the Council of Ministers. The Constitution would demand that 55% of the Member States (a minimum of 15) that represent 65% of the EU population are in agreement in order for a bill to pass. This so-called double majority increases the democracy of voting and makes the electoral procedure more comprehensible than before. In addition, decisions based on a qualified majority will cover 80% of policy areas. By this route, the Constitution would have ensured a significantly more effective EU.

A strengthening of national parliaments

The Constitution will result in a strengthening of the principle of proximity. This is the principle that the EU is not to interfere with issues which Member States can solve at a national level. The treaty strengthens this principle by giving the national parliaments the possibility to object if they believe that the proximity principle is violated. The Constitution allows a majority of at least two-thirds of the national parliaments to force the Commission to reassess a proposal, which might be in conflict with the proximity principle.

A strengthening of the people's rights

The Charter of Fundamental Rights would, through inclusion in the Constitution, become legally binding and thereby strengthen the rights of the people. In addition, the Constitution opens up the possibility for 1 million EU inhabitants to demand that the Commission put forward a bill on any given subject.

Doing away with the rotation of the presidency

The Constitution suggests that, instead of the biannually rotating presidency, the president of the European Council must serve for two and a half years, with the possibility of an extension. This is an attempt to ensure greater stability and continuity in the working of the EU. The current six-month presidency makes it hard to complete any political initiatives.